AF263231

FAVORITE FLIES

FOR

SMALLMOUTH BASS

FAVORITE FLIES

FOR

SMALLMOUTH BASS

50 FLIES FROM LOCAL EXPERTS

JAKE VILLWOCK

STACKPOLE
BOOKS

Essex, Connecticut

STACKPOLE BOOKS

The Globe Pequot Publishing Group, Inc.
64 South Main St.
Essex, CT 06426
www.GlobePequot.com

British Library Cataloguing in Publication Information available

Library of Congress Cataloguing in Publication Data available

ISBN 9780811777049 (cloth) | ISBN 9780811778145 (epub)

Printed in India

CONTENTS

ACKNOWLEDGMENTS

First and foremost, I want to thank my parents, Jim and Judy Villwock, for always supporting my dreams and introducing me to fishing at a young age. That early spark lit the fire that led me here.

A huge thank-you to Jay Nichols for giving me the opportunity to write this book and for always being there with guidance and encouragement when I needed it. To Eric Naguski—thank you for letting me use your photo studio and, more importantly, for your friendship. Tony and Chris at TCO: I can't thank you enough for always having my back and giving me the space to grow.

To all the talented tiers who generously shared their flies and knowledge—James Hughes, Russ Maddin, Alex Lafkas, Blane Chocklett, and many more—your contributions made this book possible. A big thanks to Crosby Bean and Brian Smidt for helping me get many of these flies into the Montana Fly Company catalog. And finally, Allen Rupp—thank you for the info you submitted for the book and for sending me those Dave Whitlock flies. It means a lot.

FOREWORD

I first became aware of Jake Villwock after seeing a blog post about a spring creek that I have fished since I was a kid. I was curious about this "interloper" and continued to watch his significant progress trying to figure out the notoriously picky, but very large, wild trout that I had spent the better part of forty years learning their ways and fine-tuning my tactics to a point where I was relatively competent at occasionally cajoling one of them to eat my fly.

Well, after a little time, Jake moved into my little village of Boiling Springs, Pennsylvania. I was already committed to guiding for the new owners of the fly shop in town, TCO Fly Shop. At that point I had already had a relationship with TCO that started back when they had a single shop in the Reading, Pennsylvania, suburb of West Lawn. So before long, Jake and I met face to face. We immediately hit it off and spent time on the water, hanging around the house and at the bar in the Boiling Springs Tavern, spending inordinate amounts of time talking about life, fishing, and fly tying, laughing and developing what would become a true friendship with mutual respect for not only the individual, but also abilities on the water and at the vise.

Like me, Jake leans toward single-mindedness when it comes to all things fishing. Be it tackle, tactics, fly tying, fly design, boats, and all the other things that make

up an obsession to solve any angling situation that one may be fortunate enough to encounter. After all, we are fortunate to do what we do, and no one wants to do it better than Jake does. Jake's ability to solve any angling situation is one of the things that makes him the consummate angler, fly tier, writer, and fishing guide that he has become.

Jake's ability to present angling techniques and fly-tying instruction is well thought out, clear, and easily understood due to his affable personality, intelligence, and infectious enthusiasm for all things angling. Anyone who has spent a day on the water with him as a client or attended one of his angling or fly-tying presentations can attest to Jake's ability to convey ideas and techniques clearly and in a manner that makes it all fun. After all, fishing is supposed to be fun. In his first book, *Smallmouth Bass Flies Top to Bottom* (Stackpole, 2021), Jake covers an enormous amount of information, not only about fly patterns but also the biology, behavior, and forage of the smallmouth bass. This book is the modern-day bible on smallmouth bass.

This volume, *Favorite Flies for Smallmouth Bass*, will continue Jake's indelible contribution to the world of fly fishing for smallmouth bass. Jake's thoroughness in researching patterns for this book will be instantly evident to the reader. After spending time with him photographing flies for this book, I can tell you firsthand that all the bases have been covered here. In a time when there are new fly-tying materials almost monthly and tying techniques that seem to be ever evolving, Jake has brought to the reader the most up-to-date and innovative bass flies out there today.

Eric Naguski

INTRODUCTION

Smallmouth bass have been pursued on the fly for over fifty years, yet for much of that time, they were considered a second-tier species compared to trout. For decades, fly anglers focused their efforts on coldwater streams and rivers, idolizing the pursuit of trout while leaving the warmwater gamefish, like smallmouth, to conventional gear anglers. But over the past decade or so, that perception has shifted dramatically.

This surge in popularity is due in part to a growing number of articles, books, and YouTube videos showcasing the power and beauty of smallmouth on the fly. But beyond the media, the real driving force is simply the experience itself. On the East Coast and throughout much of the Midwest, trout fisheries that are accessible by drift boat or raft are few and far between. Meanwhile, many of the same rivers and streams that

Smallmouth bass are a perfectly designed freshwater predator. Their tall back and powerful tail are built to close distance in a flash, pinning prey to the bottom or engulfing it whole. Every part of their body is made for speed, precision, and dominance in the water.

Deer hair bass bugs tied by some of my amazing friends. The cicada was crafted by Jeff Rowley, and the mop-leg frog by Joe Jackson. Grateful to be surrounded by such talent.

Fly lines play a crucial role in modern fly design. Choosing the right line is essential—it needs to match the specific application you're aiming for. Whether you're turning over a bulky streamer, presenting a delicate dry fly, or loading a fast-action rod quickly, the right fly line can make all the difference in how a pattern performs on the water.

Author Jake Villwock hooked up with a feisty early spring smallmouth, battling both the fish and the cold temps

lack trout are teeming with smallmouth bass—aggressive, acrobatic, and incredibly fun to catch.

In my seventeen years as a guide, I've seen countless anglers who once turned their noses up at smallmouth quickly change their mind after hooking their first smallmouth on the fly. Personally, I came from a background of striped bass and trout fishing, but I had a dream of owning a raft and floating rivers for any species I could find. As it turned out, where I lived, smallmouth bass were the untapped goldmine. It only took a handful of fish to convince me that I was onto something special—floating remote, beautiful rivers that saw little pressure and discovering a predator that rivaled anything I'd targeted before.

Over the years, like anything in fly fishing, my flies and techniques have evolved to match changing conditions and increasing pressure. But it wasn't always like this. As I mentioned, for a long time fly anglers largely ignored smallmouth. Thankfully, there were a few who didn't.

FOUNDING FATHERS

Several anglers were instrumental in putting smallmouth bass on the fly-fishing map. While many deserve recognition—names like Lefty Kreh and Harry Murray among them—three individuals stand out to me, not just because of their influence, but because I've had the privilege of meeting and learning from them personally: Bob Clouser, Chuck Kraft, and Dave Whitlock.

Bob Clouser

A native of Middletown, Pennsylvania, Bob Clouser is perhaps the most recognized name in smallmouth fly fishing. He's not only authored seminal books on the subject, but also created one of the most effective flies ever tied: the Clouser Minnow. With nothing more than bucktail, dumbbell eyes, and a bit of flash, Bob crafted a pattern that has fooled over a hundred species of fish worldwide.

On top of designing what will go down in history as the greatest smallmouth fly—the Clouser Minnow—Bob has created countless other patterns and developed innovative techniques to fish them. One that will always stand out to me is the Clouser Crayfish and the way he used to dead-drift it or fish it under an indicator. Another standout pattern is the Clouser Floating Minnow, which cleverly uses two of Rainy's foam spider bodies and bucktail to imitate a waking baitfish. His creativity and understanding of smallmouth behavior continue to influence how we tie and fish today.

What makes the Clouser Minnow so special is its adaptability. Change the size, weight, or color and it can mimic nearly any baitfish in almost any water condition. In my own fly-tying library, Bob's books sit side by side with my own, and I consider his contributions foundational. Despite traveling the world chasing countless species, Bob always returns home to fish smallmouth. There's something about them—they're one of the greatest freshwater predators on a fly.

Some of Bob's most iconic fly patterns—the Clouser Cray, the Clouser Minnow, and the Floating Minnow—have become staples in warmwater fly fishing around the world.

Chuck Kraft

Chuck Kraft, a legendary Virginia guide, fly tier, and innovator, helped define what smallmouth fly fishing looks like in the Mid-Atlantic. He fished frequently with Bob Clouser and Lefty Kreh and guided some of the most iconic names in fly fishing.

Chuck was known for his unique and deadly effective fly patterns—many of which he fiercely protected. From the Excalibur and Boga Bug to the CK Baitfish and Crittermite, Chuck's flies were engineered with obsessive detail and tested over years. He even snorkeled rivers to watch how his flies moved underwater.

Chuck's use of materials like Ultrasuede for lifelike movement and durability was groundbreaking. His Wonder Nymph gained national recognition in *Field & Stream* in 1971, and he continued innovating until his passing in 2020. To fish a CK pattern is to fish something born from decades of experience and passion.

The Kreel Tackle Company was the first company to manufacture Chuck Kraft's tails for his fly patterns. Kreel Tackle was in business from 2000 to 2007. In 2010, with help from one of his longtime clients, Richard Wyly, Chuck partnered and began working with William Heresniak and Eastern Trophies Fly Fishing. Chuck and William worked tirelessly bringing Chuck's tails back into production, far exceeding what Kreel Tackle had done in the past. Chuck Kraft passed away on March 9, 2020.

Dave Whitlock

Dave Whitlock was not only a pioneer of warmwater fly fishing, but also a conservationist, teacher, artist, and one of the sport's most beloved figures. Dave helped reshape the sport's trout-centric focus, proving that species like smallmouth bass deserved the same thoughtful attention.

I think of Dave every morning—I drink my coffee from a mug with his smallmouth

An early deer hair popper by Dave Whitlock—a true pioneer in smallmouth bass fly design.

Dave Whitlock's NearNuff Crayfish is a timeless pattern that deserves a permanent spot in every smallmouth angler's fly box. Its realistic profile and proven effectiveness make it a go-to when targeting bass in crayfish-rich waters.

artwork. A close friend of mine, Allen Rupp, learned directly from Dave and now continues tying his patterns commercially. Among Dave's most important contributions is the NearNuff Crayfish, a pattern he once said he'd fish exclusively for smallmouth if he had to choose only one.

Dave Whitlock's legacy is woven into the very fabric of modern fly fishing, particularly in how he elevated warmwater fly fishing. His deep understanding of species like smallmouth bass reshaped fly fishing's trout-centric focus, proving that warmwater species deserved the same careful attention to technique, presentation, and fly design. Through his roles as conservationist, mentor, artist, and ambassador of the sport, Dave earned his place on *Fly Fisherman* magazine's "Mount Rushmore of Fly Fishing" alongside Joe Brooks, Lee Wulff, and

Lefty Kreh. His influence continues to shape how we approach the sport today.

The NearNuff Crayfish is one of Dave's most effective and versatile fly patterns. He said many times that if he was forced to fish one underwater fly for smallmouth bass, it would be the NearNuff Crayfish. That is high praise! Dave's approach to fly design was grounded in careful study of aquatic ecosystems: he analyzed what fish eat, how they hunt, and the movements of their prey. The NearNuff Crayfish reflects this approach, making it one of the deadliest patterns for fooling fish in a wide range of water conditions.

What makes this fly so special? The materials used are simple—dubbing, flash, rubber, and hackle feathers—but it's Dave's precise arrangement of these elements that creates such a convincing imitation. When properly tied, these materials work in concert to provide the proper silhouette, shape, bulk, color, and feel to mimic a living crayfish. The weighted eyes help the fly get down to the bottom and ride hook-point up; the snag guard allows you to present it in heavy cover and structure; and then, the fly just looks and acts like a real crayfish. Stripped, twitched, or dead-drifted, the NearNuff Crayfish behaves just like the real thing, triggering aggressive strikes from fish that instinctively recognize an easy meal.

Another reason for its productiveness is its adaptability. Crayfish are found in nearly every freshwater system, and Dave designed this pattern to be fished in rivers, lakes, flowages, flats, and ponds. It can be tied in different sizes and colors to match regional crayfish variations, making it productive everywhere. Whether it's smallmouth bass in rocky rivers, largemouth in weedy lakes, redfish on flats, or a big trout looking for protein-rich prey, the NearNuff Crayfish consistently produces results.

Keeping Dave's patterns alive isn't just about nostalgia—it's about preserving a legacy that continues to help anglers catch fish and deepen their understanding of the sport. Every time someone ties or fishes a NearNuff Crayfish, they're not just using a great fly, they're carrying forward a piece of Dave Whitlock's incredible contribution to fly fishing. And that's something worth keeping alive.

A NEW ERA OF FLY DESIGN

As smallmouth bass fishing has grown in popularity, so too has the innovation behind fly design. From new materials—both synthetic and natural—to advanced tools and tying techniques, the evolution has been nonstop. Flies are now more lifelike and more durable than ever.

One of the modern innovators who continues to push the boundaries is Blane Chocklett. With his Game Changer platform, he's revolutionized the swim-fly game using articulated shanks to create unbelievably realistic baitfish imitations. Blane, along with other forward-thinking tiers like Russ Maddin, James Hughes, and Mike Schultz, have paved the way for how we target smallmouth today.

WHAT THIS BOOK COVERS

In this book, I'll break down smallmouth fly fishing into the three primary feeding zones: topwater, mid-column, and bottom. Each section will feature patterns designed for those zones, including my own creations and flies from some of the most respected guides and tiers in the country.

You'll get not only recipes and photos, but also insights into when and how to fish each fly. Many of the contributing tiers have included their own words explaining the design and tactics behind their patterns, so you're getting knowledge straight from the experts.

Topwater fishing has evolved from big, bulky deer hair poppers to sleeker, more effective foam and articulated bugs. The mid-column "swim fly" game is now defined by neutrally buoyant baitfish patterns fished on intermediate or floating lines. And at the bottom, where many big smallmouth feed, we'll dive into crayfish, hellgrammite, leech, and stonecat imitations.

TOPWATER

The size and color of your topwater flies are crucial, depending on the conditions and the size of the flies the bass are feeding on. Be sure to have a variety of options.

*F*or many anglers, topwater fly fishing for smallmouth is the ultimate experience. There's a mindset in warmwater fishing that mirrors the way trout anglers match the hatch on various streams. Topwater fishing for smallmouth, however, is much more than just tossing a popper out and hoping for the best. Mayflies, cicadas, damselflies, grasshoppers, frogs, wounded minnows—these are just a few of the food sources smallmouth will target at different times of the year.

But when it comes to smallmouth, it's often not so much about what they're eating, but how and where they're eating it. Are they stationary in the middle of the river, rising to sip mayflies? Are they at the tailouts of riffles, leaping out of the water after damsels and dragonflies bouncing around trying to find a mate? Or are they tight to the banks, hiding under trees, waiting for something big—a cicada falling from the branches, a frog jumping off the bank, or even a mouse in the shallows?

There's a unique thrill to floating down a river, scanning the shallows for a rise, a silhouette, or a fish suspended just under the surface, glowing in the sunlight. That's the beauty of topwater fishing for smallmouth. Once you find them, it's electric. Watching a fish confidently rise to sip your fly at a painfully slow pace, seeing a smallmouth explode on your popper inches from the bank before you even move it, or sight-fishing to a large fish in the shallows, gently placing your fly just feet in front of it—soft enough not to spook it, but loud enough to grab its attention—that's what topwater fishing is all about!

Early mornings are a great time to wade out and find rising fish in the summer months.

While topwater is usually a summer game, there are times in the spring and fall when it can be just as effective. Frogs are prevalent in the spring, and during the fall, baitfish can sometimes be the only thing on the menu. So, if the conditions are right, you can be throwing topwater flies for smallmouth from May all the way through October!

There are so many topwater flies out there today for every scenario. In this section, I'll highlight some of my favorites for each situation; dive into the stories behind their design, the people who created them, and the materials needed to tie them; and share some techniques on how to fish them effectively.

Ol' Mr. Wiggly

(Originator Charlie Piette; tied by Jake Villwock)

I t's no surprise that this fly is at the top of my list of favorite flies for small-mouth bass. Ol' Mr. Wiggly is an absolute must-have for summer smallmouth fishing everywhere, and it was designed by Charlie Piette of Tight Lines Fly Fishing Co. in Wisconsin.

Today's smallmouth have become wise to the old heavy, loud poppers of the past. Nowadays, we spend more time focusing on smaller, lighter, and quieter presentations to entice a strike from larger smallmouth. The loud, splashy presentations of traditional poppers almost never work anymore. When conditions are right, such as higher water levels and slightly off-color water, bigger and louder flies are still effective. However, in the low, clear summer flows we often encounter, smallmouth become highly

- **Hook:** #6 Ahrex NS156
- **Thread:** Chartreuse Danville 140
- **Tail:** Tan/chartreuse Sight Cast Marsh Legs
- **Sighter:** White Chicone's Fettuccine Foam
- **Accent legs:** Black Nymph Sili Legs
- **Body:** Tan Thin Fly Foam (2mm)
- **Front legs:** Tan/clear Sight Cast Marsh Legs

Charlie Piette's iconic fly, Ol' Mr. Wiggly, has taken the warmwater scene by storm. It's a simple yet deadly pattern that proves just how effective less can be.

aware of their surroundings, and loud presentations are no longer the best option.

Charlie spent a lot of time experimenting with Western patterns like the Fat Albert and other hopper patterns, eventually combining them to create a more purpose-built fly for the spooky fish in his home waters. I've long said that the most natural part of any topwater presentation is the initial "plop" when the fly hits the water. Bugs and critters that land on the water always cause some disturbance. There's nothing natural about the "bloop, bloop, bloop" sound of a popper being stripped across the surface.

When Charlie designed this fly, he aimed for something that sat lower in the water, created less disturbance upon landing, and wiggled without requiring a lot of movement. He wanted stealth. He wanted natural. And let me tell you, he nailed it!

Many insects that fall onto the water, like grasshoppers, moths, cicadas, and crickets, struggle to get off the surface once they land. But even if they can't take off, they'll continue to wiggle, buzz, and struggle their way down the river. This is a dinner bell for smallmouth of all sizes. I think this is why this fly works so well. Give it a subtle

Angler Dave Brooks proudly holds a beautiful summertime smallmouth, caught on a blue Ol' Mr. Wiggly that mimicked a damselfly.

twitch, and it creates a small ring of ripples around the fly.

Personally, I find a tan body with chartreuse thread to be the most productive summer color combo. However, I always keep blue, olive, yellow, and black versions in the box. With these five colors, you can imitate nearly any bug on the water. My typical Ahrex Traditional Shrimp hook size is 6 or 8, which is roughly equivalent to a size 4 in the Partridge Sedge Caddis hook I used to use. I prefer the shrimp hook because it has a slight curve, giving the fly more dimension.

My version of Charlie's fly is a slight variation, but it's the same in many ways. I add two sighters to the top of the fly to help anglers see it at a greater distance, and I also add small black rubber legs to the middle of the fly for a bit of contrast and depth. I've experimented with dubbing on the underbody like Charlie does, but for the sake of keeping the fly as slender as possible, I chose to use only thread for the body.

This fly will forever be a staple in my summertime fly box, and as of now, it outnumbers my poppers by a 4-to-1 ratio. When the going gets tough, give it a wiggle!

FISHING TECHNIQUES

This fly is meant to be subtle on the water, so most of the time I simply cast it toward the target and let it sit. Occasionally, I'll lift my rod tip a few inches to give the fly a slight twitch. During the summer months, I typically use a 10- to 12-foot leader to help it land softer. If you can see the fish, cast just a few feet in front of it and let the fly drift naturally.

Foam Scorpion

(Originator and tier Russ Maddin)

- **Hook:** #1/0 Ahrex Trout Predator
- **Thread:** Tan Veevus 6/0
- **Tail:** Yellow/black bucktail
- **Flash:** Black/orange Hareline Voodoo Fiber
- **Body:** Yellow MFC High Rise Foam (3mm)
- **Legs:** Black/gold Barred Sili Legs
- **Underbody:** Black Lively Leg Crustacean Brush (½")
- **Sighter:** Black/red MFC High Rise Foam (3mm and 2mm)

This is a bug I've become obsessed with over the years. The larger version is an incredible fly to use when the water is higher but still clear. It has the profile of a large mayfly or a small baitfish. The rubber legs from the brush, combined with the extra-long Sili Legs, give the Foam Scorpion incredible movement, even when it's sitting motionless on the water. I find it especially effective when damsels and dragonflies are floating just above the surface. While blue is always a reliable color when they're around, dragonflies come in a variety of colors, ranging from black and yellow to bright green. So, you can really experiment with different colors.

The Foam Scorpion can be a lot of different things—a bug, a baitfish—but no matter how it's interpreted, it's versatile and effective and it shines in just about any warmwater situation.

The High Rise Foam this fly is tied with ensures it stays afloat all day. I do spray it with High N Dry at the start of the day, but just a couple of spritzes will keep it floating like a champ.

I believe this fly should have a spot in every smallmouth angler's box. I fish it similarly to the Ol' Mr. Wiggly, but one thing this bug has that the Wiggly doesn't is the bucktail tail. The bucktail creates a unique profile. Because it's not a cut-and-shaped material but more of a natural, messy texture, I think the broken lines in the profile add to the fly's natural appeal.

If the regular Scorpion is too large for the conditions, there's always the option to switch to the mini version. I absolutely love the mini one. I tie it mostly in natural colors—olives, tans, and browns—but I always keep a few blue ones in the mix too. This fly performs exceptionally well when bugs are floating on the surface. The use of deer hair for the sighter is perfect, helping the fly land softer while giving you something taller to track at a distance. I pull out this fly when nothing else is working, and it seems to get results every time.

The mini version is tied with 2mm Loco Foam instead of the 3mm High Rise Foam, which gives it a nice, slender profile and a natural glow when dead-drifting. The reality is these bugs have the right profile, movement, and floatability to trick fish all day long.

Many anglers dislike the low, clear summer days on the river because smallmouth

Russ Maddin's Mini Scorpion in natural colors is one of my go-to summer flies for smallmouth.

can be spooky and tough to catch, but these are my favorite days. This is when you can pull out lighter rods and smaller tippet, fish these natural bugs, and sight-fish to picky fish. Watching a larger foam bug drift down the bank or along a logjam, and seeing an olive nose rise confidently to sip it in, is simply the best.

FISHING TECHNIQUES

I spend most of my time fishing this fly with a completely dead drift, but there are plenty of times when a short, subtle pull creates just the right disturbance to grab a fish's attention. Because the Foam Scorpion has a bullet-shaped head, you can occasionally give it a small pop. This slight movement pulls the fly under just a bit before it pops right back up, creating a soft, subtle "pop" that can entice a strike.

The smaller versions of this fly can be fished on lighter, longer leaders, but for the larger ones I try to keep the leader around 9 feet. This helps with both accuracy and the ability to turn the fly over at distance.

Oogie Boogie—Hex

(Originator and tier Russ Maddin)

There's a time and place for this fly, and when that time comes, you absolutely need to have it. Russ Maddin guides in Michigan, and one of the coolest and most epic hatches they experience is the *Hexagenia* mayfly. This giant insect emerges at night, filling both the air and the surface of the water. It's a hatch that will get just about every freshwater predator looking up.

When fishing a fly this large, it's crucial that it floats—and floats for a long time. Often, when fishing these big bugs, you're relying on sounds and feel to detect when a fish strikes. You can fish them in the early evening, but the Oogie Boogie really shines in the darkness. When I do my overnight float trips, we camp on islands, and in the summer,

The Oogie Boogie offers a perfect rendition of a Hex. The rubber legs and flash add just the right touch of realism and movement, while the foam and deer hair keep it floating for hours. It's a fly that not only looks the part but performs when it counts.

whether it's a Hex, Sulphur, *Isonychia*, or some other insect I can't even see, you can hear the bass busting large bugs on the surface. Having something as big as this is a must. It creates a significant footprint for the fish to see and feel.

The moose mane, squirrel tail, and deer body hair that make up this fly are all hollow fibers. These hollow fibers vibrate in the water, creating a sound that only the bass can detect.

Russ has come up with some amazing dry flies for both large trout and smallmouth bass around his home waters, but these flies aren't just great up there. If you're willing to fish at night, his Hex dries are something you should have with you at all times.

The subtle Krystal Flash under the tail and wrapped around the underbody is an excellent attractor for fish looking up. The foam between the stacks of deer hair not only helps the fly float, but also helps flare out the hair, contributing to the large profile that a Hex has. The Oogie Boogie will float for days, and even in the darkest conditions, it can still sometimes be visible to the angler.

When fishing at night, it's important to use a red light. This not only helps with your night vision, but it's also easier on the

The Hexagenia, *or Hex, is one of the largest mayflies in the United States, typically hatching in the late evening and throughout the night.*

During our camping trip, we heard fish rising and splashing around 10:00 p.m., so we grabbed our larger bugs and red lights and headed out. This smallmouth took a large Hex fly while it was skating across the surface.

fish's eyes, allowing them to keep feeding even if you point the light right at them (most of the time).

I consider this a favorite fly for smallmouth because even if we don't have the best Hex hatch nearby, it's still a fly that's necessary in many Midwest fisheries when Hexes are around.

FISHING TECHNIQUES

The Oogie Boogie is a trout-style dry fly fished for smallmouth, so treat it as you would if there was a 24-inch trout rising in front of you. Cast slightly upstream, give it a good mend, and try to keep it as drag-free as possible. On the other hand, at night the only way to detect a fish strike may be when your rig is under tension. So there are times when I'll cast it slightly downstream and skate it across the surface. I'll still mend it to slow down its speed, but always try to keep slight tension on it.

Pins N Needles Damsel

(Originator and tier Jake Villwock)

- **Hook:** #8 Ahrex Trout Predator Light
- **Thread:** Black Danville 140
- **Shank/junction:** Pin cut with small Senyo's Intruder Wire
- **Body:** Damsel blue MFC High Rise Foam
- **Rear legs:** Black Nymph Sili Legs
- **Front legs:** Blue/clear Chicone's Crusher Legs (regular)
- **Flash:** Blue/clear Senyo's Predator Wrap
- **Sighter:** White Chicone's Fettuccini Foam
- **Eyes:** Pin tops

The Pins N Needles Damselfly is a fly I've had in mind ever since the release of the Ol' Mr. Wiggly. While it may not be the first articulated damselfly, I wanted to take the basic profile of the Wiggly and refine it, making it smaller and narrower for a more realistic damselfly silhouette. Damselflies are typically quite slender, and many foam patterns available today tend to be on the wider side. While extended bodies made from deer hair or synthetics are great, I wanted to create something entirely from foam.

The Pins N Needles Damsel is one of my own creations—an idea that's been on my mind for a long time. It's small and articulated, designed for those times when the water is low and clear, and the fish are keyed in on damselflies. The foam keeps it riding high, while the articulated abdomen brings subtle movement, even on a dead drift.

I started tying smaller damsels using Whitlock's Gorilla Damsel-Dragonfly bodies in size small. These flies floated incredibly well, but I felt they needed a little more movement, so I added the same rubber leg configuration that I use on the Wiggly. After that, I realized the sighter needed to be more prominent. Initially, I used two tie-ins of thread, but the fly spun too much in the air due to overcrowding, so I opted for a single sighter that extended over the entire body, which worked better.

To give the fly a bit of flash and a translucent look from below, I incorporated Senyo's Predator Wrap with the rubber legs. This added just the right amount of shimmer without overpowering the design. I also borrowed a trick from Blane Chocklett's book, using the tops of pins for the eyes. I cut the pins close to the tops at an angle, making it easier to punch through the foam.

I'm a huge proponent of using lighter blue foam for damselflies, so I chose Montana Fly Company's High Rise Foam in damsel blue. It's the best floating foam I've found, and the color is spot on. For the articulated section, I wanted something lightweight with a straight eye. The lightest option I found was the rest of the pin I had cut off, which also made it easier to punch through the foam and fold it over itself. For the junction, I used Senyo's Intruder Wire in small, which is incredibly thin, allowing me to create a small junction without compromising the fly's movement.

The Pins N Needles works wonders when fish are keyed in on damselflies during the summer months. It's so light that it floats beautifully and lands softly on the water.

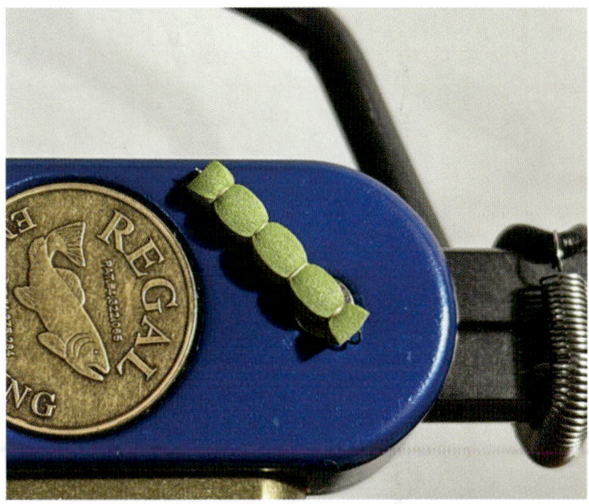

I've included photos to show the pin with the wire eye and a completed rear section, so you can see a detailed example of the abdomen.

You don't have to move it much when presenting it because the articulated abdomen and rubber legs provide plenty of natural movement.

I tie these flies in several colors, with blue and olive being my go-to choices, but I've also tied them in black, tan, red, and even orange. Although it's primarily designed as a damselfly, the same profile can be adapted for other slender insects. By adding more legs and a rubber tail, you could easily turn it into a pattern for other river bugs. I haven't tried it yet, but I plan to adapt this design into a Hex dry fly. With its extended body, the profile is already close to what I envision, but I'd likely scale it up and add a larger hackle wing to complete the look.

FISHING TECHNIQUES

I fish the Pins N Needles Damselfly in two ways. The first, and most subtle, is to cast it above the fish and let it drift drag-free to where you've seen the fish rise. With its lifelike movement, this method often entices a strike.

The second way I fish it is by giving the fly an occasional twitch. Simply raise your wrist a few inches to impart movement and life into the fly. Since it's so light, you can cast it close to the fish, whether you saw it rise or are targeting one sitting in the shallows. I always like to get the fish's attention with the fly hitting the water first—this is my go-to strategy.

A summertime smallmouth that fell to the Pins N Needles Damselfly

Damsel Boga Bug

(Originator Chuck Kraft; tied by William Heresniak)

Boga Bugs are a staple in my fly box every summer. I absolutely love the level of detail that goes into each one of these flies. William Heresniak spends countless hours bringing these bugs to life, starting from raw cork and transforming them into beautifully painted, ridiculously durable flies that, as long as they don't end up in a tree or break off, will last literally forever.

- **Hook:** #4 Mustad CK52S
- **Thread:** Black UTC 140
- **Body:** Composite cork, painted and epoxied
- **Tail:** Blue Eastern Trophies Damsel Tails
- **Collar:** Black Cactus Chenille
- **Legs:** White round rubber legs

From the mastermind of Chuck Kraft, this fly is as effective as it is a piece of artwork. Built to fish hard, the Damsel Boga Bug is incredibly durable and floats all day long. The use of cork—still the most rugged and reliable topwater material out there—makes this pattern both tough and timeless.

Chuck Kraft is a legend in the smallmouth bass world. He was the pioneer of smallmouth fishing in Virginia and took immense pride in crafting his bugs. You'll see several of his creations throughout this book, and for good reason—his flies work, they're durable, and they have the realistic triggers that smallmouth just can't resist.

The Damsel Boga Bug is a topwater fly for smallmouth bass and has been a Chuck Kraft staple for decades. These bugs are smaller and incredibly easy to cast. Size 4 Damsel Boga Bugs provide a great splash while maintaining a smaller profile. I believe the smaller profile is crucial when the water is low and clear, as it often is during the summer months. The rubber legs are placed perfectly, ensuring they don't get tangled with each other or the hook. The small suede tail adds a nice taper to the fly, and when it gets wet, it gains its own movement, becoming a bit rubberier and softer, which is perfect for enticing smallmouth.

William has maintained the same painting style that Chuck used for decades. The color combinations and segmentation, all covered with a clear finish, add a lot of dimension to the fly, making it even more lifelike.

Nothing floats quite like cork, and it will always outlast foam or deer hair. While it may take a little extra time to trim, coat, and paint, it's worth it because once it's done,

Chris Borek with a killer smallmouth that took the Boga in shallow water just before dark.

you'll never have to do it again. Unless, of course, you climb a tree or need to snorkel for them after they get stuck—that's a must!

Aside from the occasional break-off due to a bad hook set or a frayed tippet, these bugs are indestructible. I've had the same dozen flies from William for about ten years, and they still look as good as the day I bought them.

Going back to the "splat" of these bugs—while they do have some weight to them, that's part of what makes them so durable. They hit the water a little harder than most flies, but I think that's what makes them so effective. The sound they make when they land is natural for just about any bug hitting the water. It grabs the fish's attention, and once they notice, they just won't leave it alone.

I like these flies in olive and blue, but if you're thinking about trying them, you can paint them in any color combo you want. Most damsels are olive or blue, but I've seen them in red and black too. If you want to upsize them for dragonflies, you can get them in black as well—another great color for fooling those picky fish.

FISHING TECHNIQUES

To fish the Boga Bug, give it a good splat near your target area or fish, then let it sit. The legs will move, and the splash will grab the fish's attention. From there, read what the fish is doing. If it comes right up and eats it, that's the best-case scenario. If it comes up slowly and curiously, give the fly a little wiggle to show that it's alive. Once you have the fish's attention, stick with it until it either commits to eating or loses interest. Of course, we never want them to lose interest, but it happens. Don't get discouraged—just find another target and repeat the process.

Campbell Damsel Slider

(Originator and tier Allen Campbell)

- **Hook:** #6 Ahrex Light Stinger
- **Thread:** Black Danville 210
- **Tail:** Blue deer body hair
- **Flash:** Pearl Flashabou
- **Legs:** Blue/black Hot Tip Sili Legs
- **Body:** Blue/black deer body hair

Stacking and trimming deer hair is an art in itself, and Allen Campbell has been perfecting his spinning and trimming techniques for years. I'd say he's got it down to a science now! His Damsel Slider is an awesome addition to your box for the summer months. This particular fly is tied to imitate a blue damsel, but you can tie them in all sorts of colors to imitate both damsels and dragonflies. One of the things I particularly love about these extended-body deer hair bugs is how you can make them incredibly slender and add neat thread patterns for segmentation. Allen's version includes a touch of flash in the underbody, and

Pull it or pop it—this fly dives down and floats back up, creating a lifelike action that fish can't ignore. The Damsel Slider perfectly imitates damselflies or dragonflies diving to lay their eggs on submerged grass, making it a deadly choice when those insects are active.

I think this small detail really elevates the fly's effectiveness. The flash creates a subtle glisten when the fly floats on the surface, providing something extra for fish to see from below.

The rubber legs are another great feature of this fly. They provide a lot of movement—keep it still, or give it a gentle pull, and the legs will move like crazy, making the fly look alive and enticing to smallmouth.

One thing I really appreciate about this fly is its slider head. This style of head keeps your presentation light and unobtrusive. Instead of pushing a lot of water and creating a large disturbance that could spook fish, it quietly displaces water over the fly, making it dive or slide under the surface. This creates a subtle ripple effect on the water's surface without unnecessary noise or commotion.

Campbell also does something a lot of guides and tiers do with their deer hair bugs—he coats the bottom of the fly with a thin layer of UV curing glue. This serves two purposes: it makes the fly much more durable, and it ensures that the fly always lands right-side up. When fishing with deer hair bugs, water can penetrate the fly in different ways, which can cause uneven weight distribution. This can result in the fly landing heavy-side down, which isn't always the intended "bottom." The UV glue helps

Toles Hartman with a tank that was fooled by a small deer hair Damsel Slider in the early summer months.

solve this problem, making the fly land as intended, every time.

Smaller deer hair bugs, like this one, always land softly, which is crucial for those summer days when damsels are active. This soft landing allows you to cast closer to your target without spooking the fish with a big splashdown. As fishing pressure increases, so does the fish's awareness of its surroundings. As guides and tiers, we have to adapt, making flies smaller, lighter, and more natural. This is one way to outsmart those more cautious fish.

This fly might be a little larger than a typical damsel imitation, but that's okay—it's still a meal that a smallmouth can't resist. When damsels are around, so are dragonflies, and smallmouth aren't too picky if the fly doesn't spook them. Damsels and dragonflies don't land long on the water; a smallmouth must commit to eating them before they fly off. If the fly is the right color and in the right spot, they'll munch on it.

FISHING TECHNIQUES

When fishing the Damsel Slider, land it softly on the water, then give it a few light pulls to get it to dive just beneath the surface—and hold on! I also spray all my deer hair bugs with High N Dry to keep them floating for hours. If the fly stays afloat, the fish will keep coming for it. I never pop these flies; the key to success with this pattern is a subtle, quiet presentation. That's what makes it so effective.

J & M Cork Poppers

(Originator and tier Jeff Price)

- **Hook:** #4 Mustad CK52S
- **Thread:** Black UNI 8/0
- **Tail:** Yellow calf tail
- **Legs:** Yellow round rubber legs
- **Collar:** Olive grizzly rooster saddle
- **Body:** Cork popper
- **Eyes:** Hand-painted

I'm going to start by saying that this chapter isn't just about Jeff Price's poppers. While I'll be featuring Jeff's work, I also want to discuss a few of my other favorite cork poppers. Jeff's poppers deserve special attention because they are true works of art. Every dot, eyeball, and color is hand-painted, and that attention to detail is what makes these bugs so exceptional.

One of the things I really appreciate about Jeff's poppers, and something that connects them to some of my other favorite store-bought poppers, is their simplicity. There was a time when most poppers were designed to imitate frogs, and only frogs. But these days poppers can mimic a variety of bugs, and as long as they are tied simply, they're effective.

Cork poppers should be a staple in every bass angler's fly box. There's no need for floatant—the paint and coating prevent the fly from getting saturated, so you can fish them all day long. While many companies produce them commercially, some of the best versions come from talented tiers who take the time to hand-paint and craft their own.

Jeff's poppers have everything they need and nothing more. He uses calf hair for the tail, a simple grizzly hackle for the collar, and just the right amount of rubber legs to add movement when the fly is stationary. At first glance, you might think there are too many rubber legs, but that's part of the genius. You can easily trim a couple of legs to match the situation or leave them all intact and see how the fish react—then adjust accordingly. Once painted, Jeff coats the poppers for durability, ensuring they'll last a long time. If you really study his work, you'll gain a whole new appreciation for the artistry involved in making these poppers.

Cork poppers are ideal for summertime fishing, and one of the most popular options today is the Boogle Bug. These things are incredible. They come in three sizes: 8, 6, and 4. Personally, I find the size 6 to be the perfect choice for summer fishing, while the size 4 works great for higher water when you need a larger sound print to grab the fish's attention.

What stands out to me most about Boogle Bugs is, once again, their simple design. They feature a marabou tail, a hackle collar, and rubber legs. But what really caught my eye when I purchased these was the red dot on the bottom. I'm

Even when the trees aren't fully leafed out, you can still get fish to bite on poppers, as long as the water temperature is right. The key is to fish them slowly and keep them close to the banks.

not sure exactly what the fish see, but the number of fish that go after these poppers is impressive, and it must be due to something. I'm starting to see this red dot pop up on many other popper designs now. I'll always keep a generous supply of Boogle Bugs in my box because they just work, and they work well.

Another manufacturer of fantastic cork poppers is Montana Fly Company. They also focus on that simple design—marabou, hackle, and rubber—because, really, that's all you need. But what MFC brings to the topwater game with their Bombshell Poppers is color. They have some amazing combinations, like tan and gold, bronze, damsel olive, and green. While it may not seem like much, more-natural colors can make a huge difference on some days. Having multiple color options is essential. I particularly love the tan/gold and bronze colors when fish are shying away from bright chartreuse or yellow. Sometimes it's the subtle changes in color that can make the fish more committed rather than just curious.

Cork poppers, especially those coated with a good layer of hard epoxy, are incredibly durable. These flies can last a long time, and if they start to lose legs or collars, it's easy to take them back to the vise and re-dress them. With just a few adjustments, you can get even more life out of them.

FISHING TECHNIQUES

If you've ever sat in on one of my presentations, you know I always say, "Don't pop the popper." Pull it, twitch it—just make it look alive, but don't create too much noise. Unless the conditions really call for it, I almost never pop my poppers. I prefer to get them close to the fish, and the most natural part of the presentation is the drop. When that fly hits the water and creates a disturbance, that's what catches the fish's attention. After that, just let it sit and watch how the fish reacts.

BroodX Cicada

(Originator and tier Jake Villwock)

The BroodX Cicada is a pattern I created three years ago during one of our 17-year cicada hatches here in the Cumberland Valley. The beauty of this fly is its versatility—you can use it for the 17-year cicada hatch, the 13-year hatch, or even the annual cicada. By simply changing the foam from 2mm to 3mm, you can tie a larger, bulkier version to imitate the annual cicada.

While the 17-year cicada is smaller and slenderer than the annual, fish seem to care more about the right color and presentation than size, especially when it's

- **Hook:** #6 Ahrex Traditional Shrimp
- **Thread:** Amber Danville 140
- **Flash:** Pearl/black/orange Arctic Flash
- **Wing:** White/gray poly floating yarn
- **Underbody:** Black Thin Fly Foam (3mm)
- **Body:** Black/gray Thin Fly Foam (2mm)
- **Legs:** Amber/black MFC Barred Sexi-Floss
- **Sighter:** Orange Thin Fly Foam (2mm)
- **Eyes:** Red sawing pins

When the BroodX was making its appearance a few years ago, I set out to create a fly that was both fun to tie and effective on the water. After a few renditions, the final cicada pattern came to life—realistic, easy to cast, and deadly when fished. The fish seemed to enjoy it as much as I did tying it.

presented with small, struggling ripples on the water's surface.

The design of this fly aims to float with its belly in the water's film, while the wings ride a little higher for better visibility at a distance. To enhance visibility further, I've added a bright orange sighter on top. Rather than letting the sighter flare forward and backward, I glue the front half so it folds over the head, giving the fly a "headlights" look. This modification helps the angler see the fly much more easily from a distance, without affecting its effectiveness.

I adapted this technique from Chuck Kraft's Excalibur bugs, where he painted the sighter onto the front of the head. Initially, I doubted whether this approach would improve visibility, but when I saw how the sighter lights up in the sun, I realized I was wrong—the fly's angle makes it invisible to fish while still being easily seen by the angler.

I use Montana Fly Company's barred legs for this fly because they stand straighter, providing a more defined profile on the water, and they also create excellent movement.

George Rudy proudly holds up a beautiful smallmouth bass he caught while fishing the BroodX. Despite the high water levels, the fish were holding tight to the banks, making for an exciting and successful catch.

The amber color matches the natural cicada's legs beautifully.

For the wings, I prefer poly floating yarn because it keeps the fly afloat for long periods, even after being struck by fish. The fly holds on to floatant very well, and I treat it with High N Dry spray to extend its floatation. The subtle flash in the wing adds dimension and catches the sunlight, much like a natural cicada's wings.

Over time, I've tied this fly using various wing materials, from web wings to Blane Chocklett's Gummy Wing material. Blane has recently introduced new premade wings, which I plan to try at some point. However, I've found that omitting cut and trimmed wings doesn't affect the fly's fishability. While cut wings might look cooler, they can sometimes make the fly bulkier and more difficult to cast. Many times, I skip the cut wings and just use flash and poly for the wing instead.

The eyes are another innovation borrowed from Blane. I use sewing pins purchased from the craft store, cutting off the tops and gluing them in place with superglue. These create durable, realistic eyes without adding too much bulk. While shrimp eyes could work as well, I find them too bulky for this fly.

Overall, the BroodX Cicada is a fun fly to tie and fish. It's simple yet effective, and its design adapts easily to different cicada hatches, making it a great choice when those big, buzzing insects make their appearance on the water.

FISHING TECHNIQUES

The most natural presentation for a cicada is to mimic it falling from a tree close to the bank. Once a cicada hits the water, it struggles helplessly, unable to lift off, creating a lot of splashing and buzzing. When fishing the BroodX, I aim to make a loud "splat" as the fly hits the water. Then I let it sit and give it short, rhythmic pulls to create subtle ripples and disturbance around the fly. This mimics the struggling movement of a real cicada and draws the attention of predatory fish.

Chuck Kraft Excalibur

(Originator Chuck Kraft; tied by William Heresniak)

- **Hook:** #1 Mustad CK52S
- **Thread:** Olive Danville 140
- **Body:** Cork, cut and shaped
- **Legs:** Olive round rubber legs (large)
- **Collar:** Olive Krystal Chenille
- **Tail:** Olive CK Baitfish Tail

The Excalibur is one of the most unique, well thought-out, and durable flies I've ever fished. Designed by Virginia smallmouth legend Chuck Kraft in the early '90s, it has become a staple in my summertime smallmouth fly box. Chuck, one of the pioneers of smallmouth fly fishing on the East Coast, developed some of the best bugs I've had the pleasure of fishing. Although I haven't started tying my own yet, his legendary designs are carried on by William Heresniak, a close friend and protégé of Chuck's, who offers these flies for sale.

Chuck fished the Excalibur for over three decades, and the results remained unchanged. He was renowned for consistently putting his clients on big southern smallmouth bass. The topwater strikes you get while fishing these bugs are

Hands down, the Excalibur is the best topwater-style bug/popper you can fish for smallmouth bass. Chuck Kraft fished this style of bug for over three decades, and his clients routinely landed 5- to 6-pound smallmouth. These bugs are meticulously handmade from the finest imported and domestic cork, ensuring durability and performance every time you cast.

unbelievable. The techniques behind these flies come directly from Chuck Kraft and Walt Carey, true legends in the fly-fishing world. With eight to ten coats of paint, durable clear coats, large legs, and solid craftsmanship, these bugs don't just produce results—they last.

These flies are made from cork, coated with eight to ten layers of epoxy, hand-painted, and fitted with large rubber legs and suede tails. Simply put, you can't break them. The craftsmanship is top-notch, and these bugs are worth every penny. I've been fishing them for nearly ten years, and, I've never worn one out.

Chuck's obsession with getting these bugs to attract smallmouth the second they hit the water really shows in their design. Thanks to the weight of the foam and the epoxy layers, they create a perfect "plop" when they hit the surface, and the rounded heads make them nearly impossible to pop. This is something I really appreciate, as I prefer dead-drift or twitching presentations for my topwater bugs. Since the Excalibur doesn't have a flat or cupped face, it's nearly impossible for the angler to pop it, which keeps both me and the smallmouth happy.

William and Chuck use large round rubber legs for these bugs, which help stabilize

Summertime smallmouth can't resist the Excalibur.

them in the water, giving the fly a nice, buggy profile while keeping movement. The hand-painted patterns on the bottom of the bugs are intentional—they're designed with a segmented look and color scheme meant to attract the attention of fish. The olive, chartreuse, and white versions are painted to imitate the annual cicada, while the black ones are designed to resemble the 13- or 17-year cicada.

The eyes and sighter are painted using fluorescent chartreuse paint. The eyes face downward and forward, creating a slight "hot spot," or trigger point, that catches a fish's attention. The sighter is located on the top and forward-facing part of the fly. When the fly is 60-plus feet from the boat, the sighter stands out like a spotlight, making it easy to see, track, and pick up if you lose sight of it. William also offers kits if you want to try your hand at tying them yourself—I have a few kits sitting on my desk right now, just waiting for me to break out the razor blade and start trimming cork!

The Excalibur is a topwater bug that produces results and stands the test of time. It's a testament to Chuck Kraft's ingenuity and dedication to smallmouth fly fishing. If you get the chance to fish with one, you'll understand why it's become such a reliable fly for so many anglers. The craftsmanship, the action, and the topwater strikes make this fly a must-have in any smallmouth angler's box.

FISHING TECHNIQUES

To fish the Excalibur, focus on areas where trees overhang the bank. Let the fly ride down the bank, allowing it to settle, and wait for the ripples to dissipate. Once the rings disappear, give the fly a little pull to create more disturbance. I like to keep the fly close to the bank, so instead of stripping it back to me, I'll occasionally toss in a mend. This allows the fly to move naturally while staying parallel to the bank.

Blane's Cicada

(Originator and tier Blane Chocklett)

- **Hook:** #6 Mustad CK52S
- **Thread:** Black Danville 210
- **Legs:** Olive round rubber legs (large)
- **Underbody:** Black Wapsi Spider Body (medium)
- **Body:** Black Chocklett's Foam Skin
- **Wings:** Olive and orange Chocklett's Gummy Wings
- **Slighter:** Orange foam cylinder, trimmed in half

Blane Chocklett is known for his Game Changer platform, but he's also a master at creating foam bugs. Using his proprietary materials, Blane has crafted some killer bugs, like frogs and this cicada. To create the body, he uses two Spider Bodies, gluing them around the hook shank. This technique helps widen the profile of the bug, giving the material a stiff surface to adhere to and providing the fly with additional floatation.

Blane incorporates large rubber legs placed in realistic locations, knotted to enhance the bug's profile and movement. These oversize legs not only create life-like movement, but also help maintain the fly's floatation and keep it positioned correctly on the water.

It looks and acts just like the real thing! Blane Chocklett has been fishing cicada hatches across the United States for the past thirty years, and as he put it best, "These are the best cicada patterns I've ever used."

For the body, Blane uses Foam Skin. By cutting it into a long strip, you can wrap it forward, slightly widening each turn to create natural segmentation. The Foam Skin features a sticky back, so it adheres to itself, eliminating the need for thread to secure it. However, when you tie in the wings and legs, the thread adds durability to the fly. The wings are crafted from either Blane's Gummy Wing material or his new 3D Bug Wings, both extremely durable and realistic.

Once the fly is complete, it's a good idea to coat the thorax (where the thread is exposed) with UV glue. This protective layer helps shield the thread from the abrasive mouths of smallmouth bass or any other fish that bites down on the fly.

You can customize the body color and pattern using paint markers. Typically, I tie them in white and black, and depending on the species I'm trying to imitate, I'll paint them to match.

Like many cork bugs, this fly is incredibly durable. Not only does it look realistic, but it also hits the water with a natural splash. Thanks to the Foam Skin, it floats for hours—unlike other foams that absorb water. A quick spray of floatant and you're good to go for a long time.

This cicada is an essential fly for your box during the summer months. While the 17- and 13-year cicadas don't emerge every year, the annual cicada is consistently active in the summer heat. When a natural profile is needed, this is one of my go-to flies to fool picky fish. It may take a bit of time to tie, but like many well-made flies, it will last for seasons unless you break it off. My summer box always has at least six of these taking up space!

FISHING TECHNIQUES

Blane's Cicada is best fished close to the bank or in sight-fishing situations. I like to fish all my cicadas along banks with overhanging trees, as that's where real ones tend to land. It's not a popper, so there's no "popping" with this fly. I typically dead-drift it along vegetation, giving it subtle twitches for a more natural, living appearance.

Since this is technically a dry fly, many anglers are tempted to trout-set, or lift the rod high, when they hook a fish. I prefer a hybrid set, where I lift the rod to head height and simultaneously separate the line from the rod, creating tension without pulling the fly out of the fish's mouth.

Cohen's Frog-Leg Slider

(Originator and tier Pat Cohen)

- **Hook:** #10 Ahrex Trout Predator
- **Thread:** White GSP 200
- **Bead:** Plummeting tungsten
- **Weed guard:** 25 lb. hard mono
- **Legs:** Cohen's Creatures Frog Legs (medium)
- **Body:** Deer belly hair
- **Eyes:** Earth Fish-Skull Living Eyes (7mm)
- **Legs:** Chartreuse and olive Hareline Grizzly Barred Rubber Legs (medium)

Pat Cohen is one of the best deer hair tiers in the industry today. Not only are his flies sculpting and stacking masterpieces, but they also catch fish and stand up to the abuse that comes with being fished in tough conditions. The Frog-Leg Slider is one of my favorite deer hair flies to fish. Out of every type of topwater bug, the slider is definitely the quietest on the water. Poppers and divers create a lot of noise when you pop or pull them through the water, but the slider does just what it says—it slides across the surface, almost never creating too much commotion.

This is my favorite frog pattern. While I don't tie them myself, I'll always support my local tiers and buy these. In my opinion, Cohen's Frog-Leg Slider is the most effective frog pattern out there. Once it's on the water, it's not overly loud; instead, it slides smoothly rather than pops, making it more natural in the water.

Pat's design includes a tungsten bead on the hook bend and a thin coat of UV resin on the bottom of the fly. These two features help the fly ride slightly lower in the water column and always land with the hook point down. This means that when the fly hits the water, you're fishing right away, with no need for an extra adjustment. The UV resin coating on the bottom of the fly also adds to its durability. Smallmouth bass don't have teeth, but their mouths are far from soft. Without that coating, it doesn't take long before the fish start pulling out deer hair fibers. Once too many fibers come loose, the fly starts to fall apart. This is an important step and one that shouldn't be overlooked.

The deer hair trimming on the Frog-Leg Slider is nothing short of amazing. In recent years, I've tried my hand at stacking and have gotten pretty good at smaller things like slider heads on streamers, but topwater bugs still intimidate me. So, as I write this book, I've decided it's time to give it another go. The detail in the stacking of multiple colors to get a mottled look is incredible, but what I find most impressive is the shaping of these sliders. Cutting out the hair so the eyes sit recessed into the bug, and creating the even channel on top, helps the water flow over the back more easily.

The legs are a design Pat came up with using suede material. They're stamped out and sold in packs of six. You can dye them with clothing dye or color them with cloth markers—both methods work well and hold their color for a long time.

Pat's ability to create such detailed and functional flies is why I have so much

Cohen's Frog-Leg Slider sits low in the water and doesn't create much surface disturbance.

confidence in the Frog-Leg Slider. It's a fly that not only looks good but also works in the water, and I'm excited to give it another shot as I improve my own skills.

When you strip the fly, the water rolls over the back through a channel, allowing it to glide through the water without causing too much noise or disturbance. Fishing frogs can be incredibly addictive. It's not often that we, as anglers, get to throw such large bugs for freshwater fish, and to top it off, the fish go wild for them. Spring is a fantastic time to toss frogs for smallmouth. The frogs are mating along the banks of smaller creeks as the bass move in and out to spawn. Watching a frog land just inches from the bank, and almost as quickly as the fly hits the water, seeing a wake emerge from 20 feet away—it's hard to beat that.

As much as I enjoy fishing diver-style frogs, there's something about these sliders that feels more natural and effective. Maybe it's because they're so realistic and cool-looking, but I definitely prefer using them. I strongly believe the stealthier you can be, even with bigger flies, the more effective they will be.

FISHING TECHNIQUES

Right from the words of Pat, the slider is a lot different than a diver or a popper—it needs to be always moving to truly come to life. While you want to keep it in motion, you can and should pause it occasionally—especially if you have a curious fish following closely behind it. Those brief pauses can trigger a strike, as the fish might think the frog is just about to escape.

With the weed guards, you can fish these flies through heavier cover, whether you're working around grass, lily pads, or even downed wood. The slider will slide right over it all, making it a versatile choice for fishing in areas where other topwater flies might get snagged. This ability to handle tough cover makes the Frog-Leg Slider not only effective but also durable, allowing you to fish it in a variety of conditions without worrying about constant hang-ups.

Deer Hair
Diver Frogs

(Originator and tier Allen Campbell)

- **Hook:** #1/0 Gamakatsu B10S
- **Weight:** .020 lead-free wire
- **Thread:** Olive GSP 200
- **Legs:** Cohen's Creatures Frog Legs (medium)
- **Rear collar:** Fluorescent chartreuse Mimic Faux Feather Brush
- **Body:** Green/black/chartreuse deer belly hair
- **Legs:** Yellow/red flake Barred Sili Legs
- **Eyes:** Green plastic peg eyes (medium)
- **Flash:** Bullfrog Flashabou

Just like I did with the cork poppers, I'm going to focus on the deer hair divers. There are so many variations available today, but the original was developed by Larry Dahlberg and became known as the Dahlberg Diver. While these divers can be tied in various colors, including frog and baitfish patterns, for this chapter I'm going to concentrate on the frog-style version.

One of the most talented tiers when it comes to deer hair is Allen Campbell. His flies are tight, smooth, and incredibly well constructed. That's why I've chosen to highlight his pattern as the main

There are countless versions of this fly, but today's tiers have added some pretty awesome flair to them. Shown here, from left to right, are Allen Campbell's deer hair diver, the Dahlberg Diver, and Pat C frog diver. The traditional Dahlberg will always be the godfather of divers, but with the advancements in materials, the addition of suede legs brings both durability and a lifelike action to these flies.

example of a diver. He's also the first person I've seen put such big eyes on these bugs, and I think they look as cool as they fish. Allen is based out of the Midwest, where most of his flies don't have weed guards, unlike many others. This is mainly because the fishing in his area focuses on moving water, so there's less vegetation to worry about when fishing these flies.

In contrast to most deer hair bugs, Allen doesn't use feathers for the legs of his frog pattern—at least not in this example. Instead, he uses suede frog legs, which are incredibly durable and hold their shape well. What I love about this fly is that the head isn't too big. The taller the head, the harder it can be for a fish to get it in its mouth. The hook gap and head height on this fly are perfect.

Late spring is an excellent time to fish frogs. Here, the author proudly holds up a nice fish that took a frog in May. (PHOTO: JAY NICHOLS)

The original Dahlberg Diver is available from Umpqua Fly Company and is often sold under the name "Swimming Frog." While I enjoy tying my own flies, as I've mentioned in other chapters, I haven't yet mastered the art of spinning deer hair. So, I have no problem placing a large order for these frogs once a year to stock my box. The tail or legs are made from rooster feathers, and the fly comes pre-tied with a weed guard (which I usually cut off). What I love about this fly is its slender profile. Out of all the deer hair frog imitations I've tried, I think this one has the best balance of height and width. It gets into a bass's mouth quickly and stays there—most of the time.

The third example I want to highlight is Pat Cohen's deer hair diver. As I mentioned in the previous chapter on his slider frog, Pat's work with deer hair is exceptional across all patterns. One thing that stands out about his frog divers is the hook. He uses a slightly shorter shank hook than most, which I really like for leverage when fighting a fish. The shorter the shank, the less you need to move the rod to control the fish.

Like all deer hair bugs, these frogs are coated with UV glue on the bottom to help them land correctly and withstand abuse. The Swimming Frog doesn't come with this coating, but when I receive them in the mail, I cut off the weed guards and coat them all with glue before I fish them.

FISHING TECHNIQUES

These frogs are designed to make noise, so don't be shy—make some noise! Cast it toward the bank, let it sit for a few seconds, and then give it a good pop. The deer hair collar will trap water at the top of the fly, causing it to dive under the surface and then pop back up. If conditions are favorable, don't hesitate to make some aggressive pops. However, if the fish are more cautious or the conditions require a quieter approach, you can still fish them by pulling gently. This will allow the fly to break the surface without making too much noise, which can be just as effective.

Zudbubbler

(Originator and tier Matt Zudwig)

Matt Zudwig is a Midwest tier known for his exceptional balsawood poppers, which feature incredible artwork. In addition to his work with balsawood, he's also highly creative when it comes to foam. His journey started with cutting out shapes from sandals to make poppers, but he's since gone on to design his own popper heads, and let me tell you, they *really* work.

One standout fly in his lineup is the Zudbubbler—a fly that literally does what's in its name: it makes bubbles. What sets this fly apart is its slender profile, with a long and narrow front. This shape not only makes casting easier than with some other foam bugs, but also creates a larger surface area, resulting in a

Originally made from flip-flop foam, the Zudbubbler floats like a cork and makes plenty of noise. The legs and marabou give it constant movement, even on the pause, making it an irresistible target that's always alive in the water.

loud pop and a nice bubble trail behind it when retrieved.

The Zudbubbler is on the larger side for low summer flows, but I've had nothing but success with it during late spring and higher summer flows. In the spring, when we're fishing smaller creeks with long, grassy banks, this fly is a real producer. The slender profile and larger hook gap help keep fish hooked once they strike. Additionally, the marabou tail and schlappen collar, along with abundant rubber legs, make this fly effective even with minimal movement. When it's sitting on the water and rolling along the bank, it never stops moving, making it irresistibly attractive to fish.

You can add eyes to this fly if you want to give it a little more realism, but it's not necessary. I prefer to leave it with the matte finish it comes in. However, if you want to give it a shinier look, you can coat it with epoxy or UV curing glue to add that true "fished" appearance. One important thing I've learned is that the only UV glue that doesn't crack or peel off foam is Raid-Zap Flex. I now use that to coat all of my foam poppers.

Water temps are the most important part of early season topwater fishing. If you find a day when it's in the upper 50s to low 60s there is always a chance!

Matt also makes and sells his own popper heads in over ten different colors, so no matter what bug you're trying to imitate, he's got the right color for you. The best part about foam is that it can be painted, coated, or colored with markers, so it's like an open canvas to create the exact look you want.

On a side note, Matt has developed one of the most useful tools for tying any topwater fly with legs: a leg puller. This tool is tapered and thin, allowing it to easily cut through foam and pull the legs through the body. It creates a hole just large enough for the legs to go through, but not so big that they'll easily pull out. It works not just for foam, but also for deer hair and cork.

The Zudbubbler is an essential addition to any frog collection—quick to tie and highly effective.

FISHING TECHNIQUES

Treat the Zudbubbler like a frog. Cast it close to the bank, under trees, along grass flats, or near logjams. After it hits the water, let it sit for a few seconds, then give it one short, soft pull. This ensures that if a fish is already under the fly, you won't spook it. As you move a few feet off the bank, give it a couple good pops with a pause in between each. Then, hold on tight and enjoy the action!

Villwock's Frog Popper

(Originator and tier Jake Villwock)

- **Hook:** #2 Ahrex Light Stinger
- **Thread:** Black Danville 140
- **Tail:** Fluorescent chartreuse marabou
- **Flash:** Fluorescent chartreuse/black Arctic Flash
- **Collar:** Black schlappen feather
- **Head:** White Rainy's Pre-shaped Bass Pops (medium)
- **Legs:** June bug Skirts Unlimited Living Image Skirts
- **Eyes:** Holo. gold Wapsi Stick On Eyes ($5/32"$)

This is a simple bug, but it works exceptionally well during the summer months when water levels are lower. Over the years I've learned that bigger isn't always better, and sometimes it's better to err on the smaller side. The body of this fly is made from a Rainy's pre-shaped bass popper head in size medium. I've become a big fan of these heads because they feature a flat bottom, which I think gives the fly a more natural profile. It also provides just the right amount of pop for the size of the head.

There are so many premade popper heads on the market that seem either too small or too large, are too brittle, or

Tied in line with my recent obsession with airbrushing, painting, and coating foam popper heads, this fly was my answer to the hard-to-find Boogle Bug. It has a simple profile and lands softly on the water—perfect for wary fish. Change up the color, and you can imitate just about any topwater bug. The Frog Popper is versatile, fun to make, and even better to fish.

don't hold color or UV glue well. But these Rainy's popper heads have checked all the boxes for me, and they've become a staple in my tying arsenal.

I've grown fond of the Boogle Bug–style poppers because of their simplicity: a few legs, a short tail, and a collar of hackle—nothing more. The size 6 popper is the perfect size for summer months; the size 4 can be a bit large, and the size 8 might be too small for most applications. The Rainy's heads are nearly identical in size to the size 6 Boogle Bugs, so now when Boogle Bugs are hard to find, I've got a large stock of foam heads that I can color and paint to stay stocked up throughout the summer.

I appreciate simplicity when it comes to poppers. I believe you can mimic a variety of topwater food sources just by adjusting color and size, rather than complicating things with all sorts of feathers and legs. This particular popper was designed for low, clear spring days when the frogs are nestled in the banks but the fish are a little spooked and won't take a large deer hair frog without getting scared. However, I tie these in a variety of solid colors for summer months, using Copic markers and an airbrush to get the color just right. I make these poppers in shades like blue, yellow, green, tan, and white—colors that cover all the bases for what's floating on the surface during the summer.

The tail is made from a single color of marabou, but you can easily experiment with a two-tone popper as well. When I'm feeling creative, I mix it up with combinations like white and green, tan and yellow, or yellow and green—show them something new that they haven't seen before.

For the frog color, I paint the entire head one base color, then add dots and shapes to give it a more "froggy" look. After that, I've found that the only UV-curing glue that will stick to these heads and flex with the foam is RaidZap Flex. This stuff is amazing—once it's cured, you can step on the head and it won't crack or peel off.

Foam poppers are a must-have for late spring and summer smallmouth fishing. Now that I've spent the time to find what I believe is the perfect popper head, you don't have to waste time searching. Pick up a few packs of these popper heads and start tying!

FISHING TECHNIQUES

The main idea behind the Frog Popper is to be stealthy when it hits the water, but to make noise when needed. I always start with a subtle presentation, pulling rather than popping it to create disturbance without causing a commotion. However, there are times when fish want the commotion, so always pay attention to their reactions and adjust accordingly.

Typically, when fishing a frog, I try to keep it close to the bank. I cast it almost directly onto the bank and, instead of stripping it off, I mend the line to move the fly without pulling it away from the bank. Then, I pick up the slack and repeat the process every few seconds. This subtle approach can often lead to great results in shallow springtime waters where fish are more cautious.

Whitlock's MouseRat

(Originator Dave Whitlock; tied by Umpqua)

Dave Whitlock is a true legend in the fly-fishing world. His artwork has found its way onto coffee mugs, books, and the walls of tying rooms everywhere, but more importantly, Dave was a passionate lover of smallmouth bass. One of his most iconic fly designs, in my opinion, is the MouseRat. While Dave crafted many amazing deer hair flies over the years, there's something special about this mouse pattern. Primarily made up of stacked and trimmed deer hair, it floats, makes noise, and drives smallmouth bass absolutely wild.

I first started fishing mouse patterns for smallmouth about fifteen years ago. On a whim, my buddy and I decided, "Why not?" After all, smallmouth eat all kinds of things, so why not try a mouse? It only took about ten seconds of fishing

Among the first deer hair mouse patterns to hit the market, the MouseRat remains a staple in my smallmouth box. Whether it's spring or summer, few things beat the chaos that follows when a bass sees this thing skittering across the surface.

to realize that smallmouth either love or hate mice, but they eat them and eat them well. No matter the time of day, smallmouth will crush a mouse. Much like a frog, a mouse is a large, protein-packed meal that's relatively easy for a smallmouth to track and eat.

While we often hear about "mousing" for trout at night (which does seem to be the best time to get them to eat such a large meal on the East Coast), smallmouth are opportunistic predators. If a meal is available, they'll take it, regardless of the time.

Dave truly knocked it out of the park with the MouseRat, designed to imitate small rodents, like mice, or juvenile mammals that might accidentally fall into the water. The pattern mimics the movements of a struggling or swimming rodent, making it especially effective when smallmouth are keyed in on larger food sources.

The MouseRat features a tail and ears made from suede, adding durability that will outlast the fly. The whiskers may not be necessary for the fish's sake, but they add incredible realism. The eyes are made from Mono Eyes, cut and stuffed into the deer hair and secured with superglue. This fly is versatile too—Dave fished it in various sizes for a wide range of fish, including pike, trout, smallmouth, and peacock bass. When fishing these species, you're often dealing with heavy cover—from lily pads and logjams to dense grass. That's why the MouseRat comes with a built-in weed guard, though I personally trim mine off since I typically fish in areas with minimal obstacles for a topwater fly.

What I love about the MouseRat is not only its realism but also the fact that smallmouth absolutely destroy it. Regardless of the season, I always keep a few of these in my fly box. While the pattern can be a bit large for normal low summer flows, if the water is up and clear, or it's late spring, don't hesitate to cast this thing right up to the bank. One of my favorite tricks is taking it out at night on camping trips and swinging it for smallmouth. It can be incredibly effective!

Whether you're fishing clear water or targeting smallmouth at night, the MouseRat is a must-have in your fly box. It's a powerful tool for any angler looking to target these aggressive predators.

FISHING TECHNIQUES

I like to fish the MouseRat slightly downstream, allowing it to swing across the current. As it swings, I'll wiggle the rod tip to create a secondary ripple that adds to the movement of the fly. If I want to slow it down, I'll throw a small stack mend toward the fly. This helps to slow it down just enough if a fish is following it. Another effective method is to cast the fly toward the bank or any structure and gently strip it back, mimicking a struggling mouse running out of energy.

- **Body:** DCone Shaped Cork
- **Collar:** EP Streamer Brush - Red
- **Tail:** Kreinik Flash - Silver
- **Underbody:** Lead Wire - .025
- **Hook:** Mustad CK52S sz. 1
- **Thread:** Danville 140 - Red

Topwater Kreelex

(Originator Chuck Kraft; tied by William Heresniak)

The Topwater Kreelex is yet another brilliant creation from the mind of smallmouth legend Chuck Kraft. Chuck knew smallmouth, and more importantly, he knew exactly how to make them eat. The Topwater Kreelex is a floating version of one of Chuck's other masterpieces, the Kreelex—a fly I consider to be a flashy, softer take on the Clouser. And while it might be a twist on a classic, man, does it work. The Topwater Kreelex is a killer fly in its own right, and like all of Chuck's patterns, it's built to last and floats for days.

One of Chuck's trademarks was using cork as the body of his flies. He would coat and paint it so that it wouldn't crack or break—a signature technique that helped make his flies both durable and effective. Even though Chuck is no

Mirrored from Chuck Kraft's incredibly effective Kreelex Minnow, this fly is as durable as it is deadly. Fish it dead-drift, pop it, or strip it—either way, fish will go crazy for it.

longer with us, his legacy lives on through his son, William, who continues to tie all of Chuck's flies to this day. I've bought the tying kits to make these flies myself, but I often find myself picking up a few more whenever I see William at a show. Their durability is unmatched—I haven't had to replenish my stock yet.

As William puts it, "The Topwater Kreelex has been our best-producing topwater pattern since 2011, and no surprise, it's also one of our best-selling patterns and tying kits. Deadly on smallmouth bass, largemouth bass, redfish, sea trout, and more. When fished correctly, this pattern is a fly fisherman's floating crankbait. A 'wobbling' slider pattern that will bring strikes from 6 to 10 feet away and make smallmouth do 180s, coming in hot to eat."

From personal experience, I can tell you William isn't just trying to sell more flies—this fly does exactly what he describes.

I personally prefer the smaller sizes during the summer and fall when smallmouth are foraging on smaller bait and the water levels are lower. The Topwater Kreelex is especially deadly because it can produce an amazing swimming action while allowing you to fish it slowly, pausing for extended periods. Over the years I've noticed that during summer, when smallmouth have plenty of food to choose from, the bigger fish aren't always willing to chase fast-moving flies. So, when the poppers aren't working and the damsels aren't flying, I toss out a Topwater Kreelex and work it slowly back to the boat.

On a side note, when fishing smaller baitfish patterns in the summer, I prefer using a floating line. This allows me to pause the fly and not worry about an intermediate line sinking the fly too quickly. But back to the Topwater Kreelex . . .

The tail is made from Kreinik Flash, a material that has better movement than Krystal Flash. It consists of multiple fibers of varying widths and thicknesses, giving it a lot of natural movement in the water. The collar is a Just Add H2O streamer brush in a half-inch size with a dirty red color, resembling gills and creating the appearance of a struggling baitfish. The head is made of cork, shaped carefully by the tier. The shape is important, as it dictates how the fly swims and moves in the water.

FISHING TECHNIQUES

Start by tossing the fly toward the bank or any underwater structure. Let it sit for a few seconds, just in case the initial "plop" catches a fish's attention. Once you feel confident, give the fly a hard but controlled strip. This will make the fly dive just beneath the surface and slide to one side or the other. Once it returns to the surface, repeat the action until either a fish strikes or you run out of fly line.

Depending on the mood and interest of the smallmouth, you can adjust your strip speed. Try a harder, quicker pull for a more aggressive retrieve or a softer, longer pull if you want to entice them without startling them. The key is to get their attention without scaring them off.

Mini PopRock

(Originator and tier Jake Villwock)

The PopRock is a fly I designed a few years ago with a specific goal in mind—to catch stripers and amberjacks on the surface. I needed a larger fly, tied on a 5/0 hook, using the biggest popper head Flymen Fishing Co. made. It needed to be light enough to cast into the wind but still have a big profile and create a loud pop that would grab the attention of these hard-hitting fish. After seeing the reaction to the fly from stripers, amberjacks, and even redfish in windy conditions, I knew I had something special. But it wasn't until I decided to downsize it and target picky smallmouth that the Mini PopRock was born.

The Mini PopRock is tied on a size 6 hook with the smaller popper heads, which allowed me to keep the fly light enough to land softly on the water while

The PopRock is an all-around topwater baitfish pattern. The first fish to strike this fly, much like some of my other warmwater flies, was a striped bass. After that, I tied it smaller for summer and fall smallmouth—and it's proven to be just as deadly.

still making enough noise to get a smallmouth's attention.

I've always had a love for tying with bucktail; it was one of the first materials I used when learning to tie saltwater flies. So, it's no surprise that bucktail is a staple in many of my fly designs. It sheds water easily, but when wet, it creates a full-bodied profile that is perfect for attracting fish. Another material I love to use is rooster feathers. The way they move in the water gives a natural, fluid motion that I find incredibly effective.

The body of this fly is a blend of feathers and bucktail, but I can't resist adding a little flash. I like to use peacock herl, as it provides a subtle accent that helps create a more realistic look. Since baitfish are often

No, this isn't a smallmouth, but as mentioned, the PopRock was originally designed for stripers and amberjacks before I downsized it for smallmouth. (PHOTO: JEFF COEN)

darkest on their backs, this small touch of peacock herl works beautifully to mimic that natural coloring.

One challenge I've always had when tying with popper heads is the gap left between the head and the body, especially when materials like bucktail and feathers are used. To address this, I came up with a solution—I use arctic fox and reverse-tie it, so the tips face forward. When I push the popper head onto the hook, it captures the fox and pushes it back, but the tension from the material facing forward fills the gap between the head and the body. The dense butts of the fox fur also act as a small dam, keeping the material elevated when wet, which helps maintain the fly's profile in the water.

Now, when it comes to the popper heads, that's where the real fun begins. For years I struggled with airbrushing popper heads and getting that perfect glossy finish. After testing nearly every UV glue on the market, I finally found RaidZap Flex. It dries tack-free, holds its shine, won't break or peel off the foam, and—most importantly—doesn't cause the color to bleed before curing. It's a total game changer.

I don't go overboard with the airbrushing, but I do like to blend colors. I keep the underbody of the head white and gradually blend in other colors, then finish with a darker tone down the center of the top of the head. This creates a smooth transition that complements the color changes in the bucktail and peacock herl, giving the fly a natural, multidimensional look.

The PopRock is a versatile fly with a big impact. Whether you're targeting smallmouth or a range of other species, this fly's unique action and design make it a must-have in your fly box.

FISHING TECHNIQUES

The PopRock is a popper, by definition, and in many of the saltwater applications, I fish it with an aggressive pop. However, when targeting smallmouth, especially in the conditions where this fly thrives, I prefer to keep the popping subtle. Instead of sharp, aggressive pops, I focus on gentle pulls. The water gets caught in the cup of the popper head and pushes the fly to one side, or it simply pushes water around the fly, creating a small amount of noise. This slower, more methodical approach works wonders for getting smallmouth to find the fly and commit.

I find this fly works best in late summer and fall, when the fish are more focused on larger, slower-moving prey. I like to fish it around wood and large rock structures where smallmouth tend to hang out.

SWIM FLIES

Choosing the right color for the conditions is crucial when fishing swim flies. Always keep your go-to confidence colors on hand in a variety of sizes—you never know when a size change will make the difference. But don't be afraid to throw in a few wild cards too. Sometimes an unexpected pop of color is exactly what triggers the strike.

"*S*wim flies" is a term we use for baitfish streamers—flies that are meant to be stripped and retrieved by the angler. The angler manipulates the fly to create a lifelike action, making it look like a wounded or confused baitfish. Typically, most swim flies are unweighted or neutrally buoyant, allowing the angler to stall, pause, or hang the fly in the current, giving the fish a chance to catch up, get its attention, or entice a strike. However, many swim flies do incorporate weight in various forms. Whether it's a tungsten bead threaded onto the hook, lead eyes tied at the front of the hook, lead wraps around the hook bend to create a keel, or strategically placed tungsten shrimp bodies on the hook shank, all of these elements help achieve the desired swimming action for both the tier and the angler.

Baitfish patterns come in many sizes and colors, but the goal is always to imitate a wounded or disoriented minnow. White is a classic and popular color for baitfish patterns because it's easy for the fish to see and just as easy for the angler to track. Many times, when fishing a swim fly, the smallmouth will attack from behind. They open their mouth, flare their gills, and with explosive forward motion, they suck in the fly. This can cause slack in the presentation as the fish swims toward you. When fishing a darker, more natural fly, there are times when the angler may not feel the initial strike. For this reason, using white or brighter colors can help with visibility and strike detection.

That being said, there are plenty of situations where you need to fish a more natural presentation. In those cases, relying on feel is crucial. A slightly heavier or weighted fly can help with strike detection, as the weighted fly naturally sinks away from the angler, creating tension on the line—even when you're not actively stripping. If weighted flies aren't an option but you still need a natural presentation, consider adding a "tracer" to the fly. This

A fine example of why we fish baitfish flies for smallmouth bass

Smallmouth of all sizes can't resist larger baitfish patterns during the spring and fall. These baitfish are often the primary food source during these seasons, and the bass are eager to bulk up after winter— or in preparation for the colder months ahead.

term, which I learned from Mike Schultz of Schultz Outfitters in Michigan, refers to adding a small amount of white or bright-colored material to the fly to help track its movement through the water. Mike often used white rubber legs for this purpose.

Baitfish patterns should be a staple in every angler's fly box, but they're especially crucial during late winter, spring, and fall. Smallmouth feed on baitfish year-round, but they're most productive for the angler during their most aggressive periods. This begins in the spring, after a long, low-energy winter. Once the fish are hungry and migrating to their spawning grounds, they become territorial and aggressive. Similarly, in the fall, as the water cools and the bugs disappear, smallmouth are on a mission to pack on calories for the winter, turning back to chasing larger meals.

In this section, I'll share some of my favorite baitfish patterns for smallmouth, ranging from smaller, more subtle flies to large, aggressive ones.

Smallmouth tend to go after bigger meals in the spring and fall. Client Lou Nappi and guide/author Jake Villwock display a beautiful smallmouth that took a 6-inch baitfish fly. (PHOTO: BRIAN HEPLER)

Roamer

(Originator and tier Jake Villwock)

The Roamer is a fly I take immense pride in. It's one of the first flies I ever truly developed, and the story behind it makes it my all-time favorite.

About ten years ago, I was fishing for striped bass with my dad. He was catching them left and right on a 4.5-inch pearl rubber fluke, while I couldn't catch anything, no matter what I threw. That night, sitting at my parents' kitchen table, I tied

- **Shank:** 12mm Spawn articulated shank
- **Thread:** Fluorescent chartreuse Danville 140
- **Tail:** Grizzly and white rooter saddle over bucktail
- **Flash:** Pearl yellow Flashabou
- **Rear hook:** #4 Ahrex Light Stinger
- **Underbody:** Pearl Palmer Chenille (small)
- **Body:** White bucktail
- **Overwing:** Yellow Senyo's Laser Dub
- **Front hook:** #2 Ahrex Minnow
- **Junction:** Large black Senyo's Intruder Wire with 8mm red 3D bead
- **Underbody:** Pearl Palmer Chenille (small)
- **Body:** White bucktail
- **Collar:** Pepperoni Senyo's Aqua Veil
- **Pec fins:** White Barred Sili Legs, four on each side
- **Flash:** White Ripple Ice Fiber
- **Head:** Yellow and white Senyo's Laser Dub

The Triple Roamer is the result of years of R&D on the water. Originally a single-hook fly that moved like a rubber swimbait, I just couldn't leave well enough alone. From that, the Triple Roamer was born—a tail shank, hook in the middle, and hook in the front allow the fly to swim beautifully while minimizing fouling.

a fly that vaguely resembled the profile of that rubber fluke. It was a mess, but to my surprise, it worked. I caught fish with it the next day, sparking a design journey that I still don't think is over for this fly. I named it the Roamer in honor of that day. My dad has been a commercial fisherman my whole life, and the boat I spent most of my childhood fishing on was named "Roamer." It seemed fitting that this fly carry the same name, a tribute to those memories spent fishing with my dad.

Over the years, the Roamer has evolved. What started as a single-hook 4-inch fly for striped bass has transformed into a sub-2-inch fly for saltwater species and summertime smallmouth, and even into triple- and quad-articulated versions for muskie and pike. After countless trials and errors, I learned how to make a fly truly "swim." I designed the Roamer to glide side to side, mimicking the motion of a rubber swimbait, but kept it lightweight by carefully controlling my material proportions. This makes it a fly you can fish all day long without tiring.

The Roamer is a versatile baitfish pattern that works well in the spring and fall in larger 4- and 5-inch sizes, and is highly effective in the summer in smaller 2- and 3-inch sizes.

I also wanted it to have a three-dimensional profile—more like a carrot than a knife. This shape allows the tension from moving water to help move the fly as it's fished. I incorporated mostly internal or hidden flash to give the illusion of a hollow baitfish, making it appear almost translucent in certain light conditions.

The version displayed here is the Triple Roamer. This fly features a small, 12mm shank to which the tail is tied, and two hooks for added movement. The tailing shank helps reduce fouling during retrieval. If you use the second hook for the rear and place the shank in the middle, the hook tends to be too heavy, which causes it to whip forward and catch the front of the fly. This Triple Roamer measures around 4 inches, roughly the same size as the original single-hook version, making it the most versatile freshwater size in my opinion. It's particularly effective in the spring and late summer when smallmouth are keyed in on baitfish.

FISHING TECHNIQUES

To get the most motion out of the Roamer, give it a strong strip with your off hand, then pause for about three seconds. This will allow the water to catch the front of the fly and push it to one side, creating lifelike movement. It's especially effective when smallmouth aren't aggressively chasing flies on fast retrieves, making it ideal for slower presentations. When you pause the fly, it helps to pull the rod tip to the right or left to direct the fly in the direction you want it to go, further enhancing its natural movement.

- **Thread:** Fluorescent red UTC 140
- **Rear hook:** #6 Ahrex Gammarus
- **Front hook:** #2 Ahrex Trout Predator
- **Shanks (from tail to front):** Three 10mm shanks, two 15mm shanks
- **Tail:** Natural barred chickabou
- **Body:** White hen saddle
- **Underbody:** Pearl Chocklett's Filler Flash
- **Head:** White craft fur, reverse tied
- **Eyes:** Silver holographic (6mm)

Game Changer

(Originator and tier Blane Chocklett)

The Game Changer and its variants have truly changed the game when it comes to smallmouth bass fishing. Blane Chocklett has been developing this fly for years and he keeps coming up with new ways to tie it, whether it be a specific material or shank configuration. He has designed this pattern in variations from a 2.5-inch Micro Finesse Changer up to a 14-inch muskie-style Changer. The Game Changer isn't so much a fly but a platform that you can tie just about anything on. I think that's what makes this fly so amazing—that and fish kinda like it too!

For smallmouth bass I am partial to the Finesse Changer for the summer months when the water is low and clear and smallmouth can be easily spooked when larger flies enter the water. The

Created by Blane Chocklett, the Game Changer is more than just a fly pattern—it's a versatile platform that offers endless opportunities for customization and innovation. One of my favorite variations is the Feather Changer, shown in the photo, which adds incredible movement and realism to the design.

The Jerk Changer, Feather Changer, and Finesse Changer (top to bottom) are the three main variations I use for smallmouth bass.

small ones are also great to fish on a floating line because you can fish them slow and in shallow water, but with the weight of the shanks and hook, it still gets down into the strike zone and stays there.

My favorite variation of this fly is the Feather Changer, which is featured in this chapter. The Feather Changer can be tied in a variety of sizes and colors to imitate just what the bass are chasing on any given day. I personally prefer an all-white or tan and white fly. The all-white fly is easy for the angler to see, and even easier for a smallmouth to see. As I mentioned in the introduction, smallmouth bass prefer to hunt with their eyes, so making something easy to see is important. Smallmouth will also, unlike many predators, eat from the back of

The Game Changer is a deadly fly to have in your arsenal. It swims with action no matter what you do—strip it fast or slow, or just let it pause—and it drives smallmouth absolutely crazy.

the fly. This often creates slack in your fly line, so seeing a fish eat is important when streamer fishing; otherwise, you might not feel when they eat. The tan and white works great when the water is on the clear side, and you need a more subdued color to not spook them.

One of the greatest things about this fly is its lifelike movement in the water: with so many small articulations, these flies just undulate in the water like a real fish. Another great feature of this fly is the endless color options you can achieve just by changing the color of one material, or by tying them in all-white and coloring them with markers to imitate a specific bait.

Other variations of this fly include craft fur, polar fiber brushes, mallard flank feathers, and the Jerk Changer. The Jerk Changer is tied with the same synthetic materials as the Finesse Changer—it just has a lightly different shank configuration to help it "jerk" around in the water.

Later in the book we will discuss some of Blane's other variations of the Game Changer platform with some of his bottom-bouncing flies. This chapter is specific to his baitfish variations.

FISHING TECHNIQUES

It's a baitfish, let it swim. A continuous strip can work well with this fly because it already has a lot of movement on its own. However, if you really want to drive a smallmouth nuts, give it a hard strip and pull your rod tip to the right or left, then pause. This will allow the fly to rise and fall or glide side to side, removing all motion from the fly. Smallmouth love eating on the pause or when the fly isn't moving. Watch what the bass are doing and start the cat-and-mouse game with them. This fly will fool them every time!

Lafkas Brush Head Deceiver

(Originator Alex Lafkas; tied by Jake Villwock)

This is a fly that I was introduced to by one of my guides. He was looking for a fly that was easy for clients to cast but didn't give up any movement in the water. When talking with Alex Lafkas about his fly, he mentioned exactly that: "The Brush Deceiver was tied because I was looking for a fly that the action was easy to duplicate and caused less fatigue

- **Shank:** 12mm Spawn articulated shank
- **Thread:** Tan Danville 140
- **Tail:** Ginger rooster saddle with pearl Palmer Chenille covered with bleached ginger hen saddle
- **Rear hook:** #6 Ahrex Light Stinger
- **Underbody:** Pearl Palmer Chenille (small)
- **Body:** Bleached ginger hen saddle
- **Front hook:** #2 Ahrex Minnow
- **Junction:** Large black Senyo's Intruder Wire with 8mm red 3D bead
- **Underbody:** Pearl Palmer Chenille (small)
- **Collar:** White bucktail
- **Body:** Cinnamon and white craft fur
- **Head:** Redfish Flash Blend Baitfish Brush (1"), trimmed to ½"

The Brush Head Deceiver was first introduced to me by my buddy Brendan. It's the perfect swimming baitfish, with all the right materials that make it not only efficient to tie but also incredibly effective when fished.

for the angler. As a guide, both things are extremely important."

The fly displayed is the smaller version, coming in around 4 inches, but it can be tied up to about 8 inches in length. This adds even more value to the pattern as a predator fly because of its adaptability to changing conditions: when the water is low and clear but the fish are primarily feeding on baitfish, it can still be a great option, but when the water is on the higher side and you really need the noise of the material to catch their attention, a larger fly will do that.

Being tied with a mix of natural and synthetic materials, this fly has a great sound print in the water. Bucktail is a hollow material and can create lots of noise underwater. Having a fly that you are confident in is important when fishing in any conditions, and when this fly is tied properly, it just catches fish.

Being able to change the colors of any confidence fly is a huge thing when it comes to fishing different conditions. Alex mentioned that as well: "Some other factors that I really like about it are its durability and ease at which any color combination can be achieved with a small amount of craft fur."

Light weight, customization in size and color, and movement are three major factors of flies I have in my box—this fly has it all!

FISHING TECHNIQUES

According to Alex, the design of his Brush Head Deceiver allows for movement with very small rod twitches or short strips, which can play an important role in triggering fish. With each short strip the fly will glide side to side, and the dense brush head helps with pushback from the current. This allows the fly to undulate in the water as it's sitting still—again, creating the movement needed to entice a strike.

A great baitfish pattern with solid movement is hard to beat. Smallmouth won't leave you guessing—they'll let you know right away if it's working by how aggressive they react. Let the fish do the talking.

Bucktail WantaBe

(Originator Justin Pribanic; tied by Jake Villwock)

- **Thread:** Fluorescent chartreuse UTC 140
- **Rear hook:** #4 Ahrex Minnow
- **Front hook:** #2 Ahrex Trout Predator
- **Shanks (from tail to front):** 10mm shank, 15mm shank
- **Junction:** Large Senyo's Intruder Wire with olive 3D bead
- **Tail:** Olive and white rooster saddle hackle
- **Body:** Olive over white bucktail
- **Underbody:** Pearl Palmer Chenille (small)
- **Gills:** Pepperoni Senyo's Aqua Veil
- **Over flash:** Pearl Senyo's Predator Wrap, cut and center-tied
- **Head:** White Sculpin Flash Streamer Brush (2"), colored to match bucktail
- **Eyes:** Silver holographic (6mm)

This is a fly that I have grown to love for smallmouth bass. Tying it takes a little time, but if you tie it well and make it as durable as possible, it will be worth it.

My buddy Justin Pribanic is one of the best fly tiers and guides I know; he is super meticulous in both fields. So, when he sent me a WantaBe for my last book, I become obsessed with it.

I love tying with bucktail, although it can take some time to get used to and learn all the ins and outs of how to taper,

One of my favorite springtime smallmouth flies, this pattern may not be the easiest to tie, but the reward is clear. Watching the WantaBe swim and seeing how smallmouth react to it makes every minute spent at the vise worthwhile.

proportion control, and making it super durable. The taper is perfect for any baitfish, and you can tie it in different sizes and colors just by changing hook size and the color of the bucktail. I tie these from about 3.5 to 7 inches, which gives me options for different water conditions, locations, and time of year.

Two options you can choose to add when tying this fly are a rattle on the top of the front hook shank and lead wraps on the bend of the front hook. The weight acts as a keel keeping this fly vertical without a lot of side-to-side movement, but it also helps drop it down a few extra inches in the water column. The rattle is great if you are fishing off-color or dirty water—it gives smallmouth something else to key in on. This fly, unlike some flies like the Game Changer and Roamer, is tied in a two-dimensional plane, meaning it has sharp edges and is only tapered from the top and bottom. This gives it a more aggressive up-and-down motion, but it also allows the water to hit the entire side of the fly, pushing it from one side to the other.

Because it is tied with light bucktail, the WantaBe is awesome to cast all day long. I'm not sure where Justin came up with the name, but this fly works. It is tied with three articulations and two shanks—one 10mm for the tail and one 15mm for the middle of the body—then it has a short-shank hook in the rear and a longer light-wire hook in the front.

FISHING TECHNIQUES

Like many unweighted baitfish patterns, the WantaBe is best fished with a sinking line. My preferred sinking rate for most of my streamer fishing is an intermediate line that has a sink rate of about 1.5 inches per second. For most of my smallmouth fishing, I am not fishing very deep water. However, there are times when a slightly faster sinking line comes into play. For these situations I like to run a type 3 or 5 sinking line. This fly is designed to swim, so make it swim and the fish will eat it—hopefully!

Angler Jesse Gigler proudly displays a beautiful spring smallmouth that couldn't resist the WantaBe.

Shumaker's Shimmering Minnow

(Originator and tier Brian Shumaker)

- **Thread:** White Danville 140
- **Rear shank:** 15mm Flymen articulated shank
- **Hook:** #2 Ahrex PR320 Predator Stinger
- **Tail:** White marabou
- **Flash:** Silver ice Holographic Flashabou
- **Body:** Pearl UV Palmer Chenille
- **Junction:** 20 lb. bite wire
- **Head:** #6 Flymen Fish-Skull Fish-Mask
- **Eyes:** 3D (6mm)

The Shimmering Minnow, designed by Brian Shumaker, is the perfect summertime smallmouth baitfish pattern. Brian began designing this fly in 2012, with the goal of creating a baitfish that had realistic movement, was customizable, and was easy for his clients to cast. The beauty of this fly is that he successfully achieved all three.

The fly combines marabou for the tail and junction cover, with UV Palmer Chenille for the body. This construction allows Brian to take any color magic marker or Copic marker and customize the top to mimic any baitfish species.

Brian Shumaker's Shimmering Minnow is a fly that should be in every bass angler's box and is perfect for summertime smallmouth. Its size is ideal for matching the forage swimming with smallmouth, making it a go-to pattern for warmwater action.

The addition of a 15mm shank off the back of the hook provides extra movement, giving the fly a subtle wiggle that drives smallmouth bass wild. At around 3 inches long and tied with an Ahrex PR320 Predator Stinger size 2 hook, the Shimmering Minnow is on the smaller side of baitfish patterns. Its Palmer Chenille body becomes almost translucent in the water, creating a very natural minnow appearance that smallmouth can't resist. To finish the fly, Brian uses a Fish-Mask from Flymen, which not only protects the integrity of the fly but also gives it a more "fished" look, further enhancing its realism.

This fly is a must-have in any smallmouth angler's box, not just during the summer but also in the spring when water conditions become low and clear, making larger flies less effective. I always make sure to have at least six of these flies in my box. My favorite color schemes are olive over white, gray over white, and all white. Occasionally I'll swap out the pearl chenille for a light olive or tan base, allowing me to color the top with darker, more natural hues for a stealthier approach.

FISHING TECHNIQUES

Brian likes to fish the Shimmering Minnow on an intermediate fly line, which helps sink the fly a few feet below the surface. Since the fly itself doesn't have much weight, the intermediate line is the main factor in getting it to submerge. He typically uses a short leader, around 5 feet long, made from fluorocarbon for added sensitivity and abrasion resistance. This fly is designed to swim, so Brian uses short strips to make it jerk side to side, creating the natural rise and fall of a baitfish. Because it's a smaller pattern, you don't need to work it too hard—just a subtle retrieve is enough to make it more like a baitfish.

Thrasher

(Originator and tier Eric Hurst)

The Thrasher is a unique swim fly designed to target smallmouth bass and trout, particularly effective during the early and late season when smallmouth are deeper in the water column. What makes the Thrasher stand out to me is its use of lead eyes. Lead eyes are crucial in these conditions because they help get the fly down to where a smallmouth is holding, typically in the

- **Rear hook:** #4 Gamakatsu B10S
- **Thread:** Yellow UTC 210
- **Tail:** Yellow schlappen
- **Tail accent:** Grizzly hackle
- **Flash:** Copper Flashabou
- **Underbody:** Copper UV Polar Chenille
- **Collar:** Yellow deer hair
- **Overwing:** Yellow Senyo's Laser Dub
- **Junction:** Large Senyo's Intruder Wire with red bead
- **Front hook:** #2 Gamakatsu B10S
- **Eyes:** Orange/white/black Hareline Double Pupil Lead Eyes
- **Legs:** Pumpkin/red Perfectly Barred Sili Legs
- **Head:** Yellow Senyo's Laser Dub

The Thrasher is a newer fly in my lineup, but one that has exactly what you need to fool a smallmouth. The lead eyes help it swim a little deeper—putting it right in the strike zone and, in theory, in front of more fish.

deeper, riffly waters, especially when the water is colder (below 65°F) during their migration phase.

While lead eyes are essential for sinking the fly, Eric Hurst's thoughtful design balances them with a deer hair underbody and a bulky Laser Dub head. This combination keeps the fly elevated slightly off the bottom when presenting it at a slower speed but also prevents it from dragging, while still allowing it to maintain the slow, steady movement smallmouth seek. The fly's unique buoyancy and sink rate offer the perfect balance between staying down in the zone of interest and staying off the bottom, allowing it to remain active through the presentation.

Eric explains that the Thrasher was created to mimic baitfish found in rivers and lakes in his region. He named it after Georgia's state bird, the Brown Thrasher, due to the erratic swimming action the fly creates in the water. The fly features stacked and spun deer hair, with Laser Dub over the top, which makes it swim unpredictably. The deer hair provides buoyancy, while the

Weighted swim flies are especially effective when the water and weather are on the colder side. This nice bass was fooled by the Thrasher when air temperatures were below 45°F and water temps were close to the same.

Laser Dub sinks and holds water, making the fly swim with a "thrasher-like" erratic action that smallmouth find irresistible.

One of the key advantages of the Thrasher is its versatility. It's designed to be effective in a variety of water types and can be fished over structure with its hover action or sunk into deeper pools. Its versatility means it can take the guesswork out of choosing a fly when you're faced with varying conditions, making it a reliable option for both experienced anglers and beginners alike.

In early spring, when smallmouth are migrating and feeding in deeper, oxygen-rich waters, the Thrasher shines. Smallmouth are looking for easy meals without expending much energy, so a fly that gets down quickly but still has movement is crucial. Eric's design delivers exactly that—a fly that is both weighted enough to get to the fish and has the proper action to entice a strike.

FISHING TECHNIQUES

The Thrasher was designed to have movement in all levels of the water column, except maybe the surface. Fishing this fly on the swim in faster water, using only mends for action, drives smallmouth nuts. After each mend, pick up the slack line, keeping it tight so you know when a fish strikes or you've gotten too close to the bottom. Fishing it from a moving boat, I typically cast it at a slight downstream angle and strip it back, giving it plenty of pauses to allow the fly's head to drop and then rise again on the next strip. It's no secret that smallmouth love eating on the pause, so keep that in mind when determining the speed of the retrieve.

- **Rear hook:** #4 Gamakatsu B10S
- **Thread:** Olive UTC 210
- **Tail:** Tan barred rabbit Zonker
- **Flash:** Copper Flashabou
- **Underbody:** Light olive Arizona Simi Seal, put in a loop
- **Junction:** Large Senyo's Intruder Wire with red bead
- **Front hook:** #2 Gamakatsu B10S
- **Overwing:** Tan barred rabbit Zonker
- **Collar:** Yellow deer hair
- **Eyes:** Orange/white/black Hareline Double Pupil Lead Eyes
- **Legs:** Pumpkin/red Perfectly Barred Sili Legs
- **Head:** Tan/white Senyo's Laser Dub

Agent Scully

(Originator and tier Eric Hurst)

The Agent Scully is a swim fly designed to mimic the natural tapered profile of a sculpin, making it an excellent choice for targeting smallmouth bass, especially in late winter and early spring. Eric Hurst, the mastermind behind this fly, has designed a pattern that combines movement with a lifelike natural profile. The rabbit Zonker overwing, paired with a deer body hair collar, creates an inviting profile and allows the fly to move in a way that imitates a struggling sculpin, adding to its realism. While sculpins lack a swim bladder and typically spend their lives scurrying along the bottom, it's not out of the question for a smallmouth to strike

The Agent Scully is more of a hybrid—a swim fly at heart, but one that can also be fished low and slow. With so many smallmouth food sources resembling a sculpin, its profile and versatility make it a deadly choice in a variety of situations.

at a sculpin profile in the mid-column. A silhouette can often trigger an aggressive response from a smallmouth, as they are opportunistic predators that won't hesitate to take advantage of an easy meal.

One of the highlights of the Agent Scully is Eric's careful material placement. He designed the fly to work well whether actively retrieved or fished slowly and deliberately. The materials, when used at slower speeds or during a swing, still maintain an incredible lifelike action with minimal assistance from the angler. Like the Thrasher, the Agent Scully features lead eyes, helping it get down into the strike zone. It also incorporates flash to attract attention and rubber legs for added movement, making it irresistible to smallmouth bass.

Big fish like slow-moving meals—and that's exactly why the Agent Scully gets results. It shines when the water temps drop and fish get a little more selective. Crawl it slow and let it do its thing—those larger smallmouth won't pass it up.

I personally find this fly especially effective during the late winter months, when smallmouth are in deeper, slower waters. The subtle flash catches their attention, but it's the fly's movement—courtesy of the rabbit Zonker, rubber legs, and deer hair—that compels them to strike. The Agent Scully also excels as an early spring fly, just as smallmouth are migrating into warmer waters. With their metabolism ramping up, hunger levels increasing, and aggression rising, this fly perfectly matches their feeding patterns, making it hard for them to resist.

Eric's thoughts on the Agent Scully: "It's my take on a sculpin-style streamer. The body is tied with a Zonker strip over a dub loop of Simi Seal, which helps it tread water well while still diving and swimming with plenty of action. The head is similar to the Thrasher, made with deer hair and Laser Dub, which helps the fly hold its shape in the water and adds to its overall action."

FISHING TECHNIQUES

Even though this fly has lead eyes, it is at the base a swim fly, meant to be retrieved and manipulated by the angler. I prefer to swing the Agent Scully slowly through the deeper water in the cooler months. Once the water reaches optimal feeding temps, somewhere in the upper 60s / low 70s, I will start a more active retrieve, stripping once or twice with a short pause and then a single long strip with a short pause. Allowing the fly to fall during those brief pauses can grab the fish's attention, and from there it's a game of cat and mouse to keep the fish interested. Keep it moving until the fish commits.

- **Thread:** Danville 140, color to match fly
- **Shanks:** Two 15mm and one 20mm Chocklett Game Changer Shanks
- **Rear hook:** #2 Ahrex Saltwater Gammarus
- **Junction:** Large Senyo's Intruder Wire
- **Front hook:** #1 Ahrex Minnow
- **Weight:** Tungsten bead
- **Tail:** Marabou, color of choice
- **Underbody:** Chocklett's Filler Flash, color of choice
- **Body:** American hen saddle, color of choice
- **Legs:** Sili Legs, color of choice
- **Head:** EP Crustaceous Brush, color of choice

Leggy Boi

(Originator Mike Schultz; tied by Jake Villwock)

The Leggy Boi is a fly that took me a while to fully appreciate. At first, I thought it was just a Game Changer with too many legs. But, boy, was I wrong. This fly is worth its weight in gold.

Designed by Mike Schultz up in Michigan, the Leggy Boi was created to be fished in the early season when high and cold water tends to make fishing a little tricky. Mike needed a fly that would sink

The Leggy Boi is essentially a Feather Changer loaded with rubber legs—and while it's hard to categorize, one thing's for sure: bass can't resist it. It's also a super-fun fly to tie, which makes it a win all around.

slowly but still have movement and weight. It had to be effective around logjams, along current seams, and in eddies, while being versatile enough to handle the ever-changing early season colder waters. One of its key features is its ability to get down low in the water column when needed, but also float higher when being pulled over logjams and around rock piles.

This is where the fly really stands out. Mike, along with many other skilled tiers and guides, often talks about the "under the hood" aspects of flies. In other words, what makes the fly do what it does, and why it's different from the rest. The weight system in this fly is one of the most unique elements. Instead of using lead eyes or wrapping the hook shank with lead, Mike uses a single tungsten bead to provide weight. This allows the fly to break surface tension with ease and sink slowly, offering the angler better control over how the fish reacts to the fly. You can even add keel weight by wrapping lead around the bend of the hook—something you can do either at your tying bench or on the water. The beauty of this is its adaptability: you can add or remove weight depending on the situation.

The Leggy Boi is a mix of two of Mike's favorite flies for targeting smallmouth: the

Angler and friend Rob Thrash proudly holds up one of several smallmouth that couldn't resist this yellow leggy fly on a cool, damp spring day.

Game Changer and the Woodsman. The crazy number of rubber legs and the fly's articulation give it an impressive range of movement, whether it's being actively retrieved or sitting still along a current seam. Mike favors brighter colors in the spring when smallmouth are more aggressive. This also makes it easier for anglers to track the fly and spot when the fish takes the bait.

FISHING TECHNIQUES

The Leggy Boi is a swim fly, and it's built to move. Long strips followed by an abrupt stop create a dynamic action in the water, forcing it to hit the front of the fly and kick it side to side. The weight in the head helps the water push over the fly, giving it a subtle diving action that mimics a natural prey movement.

In colder temperatures, you can fish the Leggy Boi more delicately by mending the line and picking up the slack. This technique works especially well when you want to keep the fly on the edge of a current seam. It gives the fly plenty of action without pulling it out of the line you're trying to fish. Mike prefers fishing it in front of the boat. This setup not only gives you more time to fish the fly, but also increases the hookup rate.

Foxy Popsicle

(Originator and tier Jake Villwock)

The Foxy Popsicle is a streamer I originally designed for winter trout fishing, particularly when targeting slack water near logjams and current seams surrounded by faster-moving water. My goal was to create a fly with excellent movement, a natural fishy profile, and enough head weight to dive immediately when it hits the water. In these conditions, you're often working with a narrow window, usually about 10 feet,

- **Thread:** Danville 140, color to match fly
- **Tail shank:** 15mm Chocklett Game Changer
- **Tail flash:** Gold Ripple Ice Fiber
- **Rear hook:** #4 Ahrex Light Stinger
- **Junction:** Large Senyo's Intruder Wire with 3D bead
- **Front hook:** #1 Ahrex Minnow
- **Weight:** Lead eyes (medium)
- **Tail:** Four rooster saddle feathers
- **Underbody:** Tan UV Palmer Chenille
- **Under collar:** Deer body hair
- **Over collar:** Mallard flank
- **Overwing:** Tan Arctic fox fur
- **Collar:** Tan EP Foxy Brush (1.5")
- **Legs:** Sili Legs, color of choice
- **Rattle:** Glass (3mm)
- **Head:** Coyote EP Foxy Brush (1.5")

The Foxy Popsicle is a weighted baitfish pattern I came up with specifically for fishing higher water. I tie it in tan, olive, black, and white to cover a range of conditions and forage profiles.

before the fly drifts out of the strike zone and the fish lose interest.

After seeing success with this fly for trout, I quickly realized its potential for smallmouth bass as well. In spring, especially when you may only get one shot at a hole, the need for a fly that gets down quickly is crucial. You can tie it with smaller lead eyes if you prefer a slightly more buoyant presentation. The fly features two small collars of bucktail, which help keep it neutrally buoyant, though not enough to keep it from sinking. Beneath the head is a small 3mm rattle, adding a subtle noise to the presentation. The tail feathers function as a rudder, giving the fly a natural swimming motion in the water.

I typically tie the Foxy Popsicle in natural colors such as white, tan, and olive. While you could experiment with more-vibrant colors, I stick to these to entice strikes from wary fish. The rubber legs not only provide added movement on the fall but also act as pec fins, adding further realism to the fly's action. The three collars are made from 1.5-inch EP Fox Brush, a material I swear by for both smallmouth and trout streamers. These flies tend to take a beating, not just from the

Angler Andy Ellis landed this beautiful pre-spawn smallmouth on an olive Foxy Popsicle. In the early spring, when the water is still cold, it's crucial to keep the fly lower in the water column to entice these sluggish fish.

fish but from the structures you're casting around, so durability is key.

Tied similarly to my Roamer pattern, the Foxy Popsicle incorporates internal flash for a glowing effect underwater, while keeping the exterior simple and flash-free. This gives the fly a more natural, understated look, which is often what it takes to get those selective fish to commit.

FISHING TECHNIQUES

Designed to have natural movement on the fall, the Foxy Popsicle starts fishing the moment it hits the water. With weight concentrated at the front, it's engineered to dive immediately, while the slightly stiffer feathers in the tail help keep the fly swimming. Whether you're stripping it fast away from the bank or structure, every time you pause the strip, the fly will nosedive and then rise back up. It's not intended to be a suspending fly, but rather a baitfish that quickly drops into and around structure— where fish are often lying in wait, ready to ambush.

- **Rear hook:** #4 Ahrex Trout Predator
- **Tail:** Saddle hackles with flash
- **Flash:** Flashabou of choice
- **Rear body:** Pearl Senyo's Predator Wrap and hen saddle
- **Overwing:** Mallard flank
- **Front hook:** #2 Gamakatsu Worm (round bend)
- **Connection:** 40 lb. Rio Bite Wire with three 6mm plastic beads
- **Rattle:** Glass (5mm)
- **Connection cover:** Flashabou of choice
- **Front body:** Hen saddle, followed by pearl Senyo's Predator Wrap trimmed and wrapped through rattle
- **Collar:** White Marabou, wrapped tip first (two or two and a half wraps max)
- **Flash:** Flashabou of choice
- **Wing:** Grizzly hackle, one on each side
- **Throat:** Red Palmer Chenille
- **Head:** White Rainy's Foam Diver Head (small or medium)

Swinging D

(Originator and tier Mike Schultz)

Designed by smallmouth expert Mike Schultz, this fly has evolved over time to become a versatile and essential tool for anglers. Originally tied as an articulated fly with two hooks, it has since been streamlined into a single-hook pattern with a small shank off the back for finesse, clear-water situations. The Swinging D 2.0 is the next step in its evolution, blending elements

The Swinging D is one of Mike Schultz's most popular and effective fly patterns. He ties it in a variety of sizes and colors, making it adaptable to different conditions. The foam diver head adds resistance and creates enticing movement when fished on an intermediate line—perfect for triggering aggressive strikes.

of the Feather Changer and the original Swinging D.

The foam diver head is a key feature, with its elongated nose and flared collar that help "drive" the fly side to side as water impacts it. This creates a unique, dynamic action that mimics the motion of a distressed baitfish. The marabou collar adds additional movement, especially when the fly is stalled in the water. Meanwhile, the tail feathers direct the water around the back end of the fly, giving it fluid, lifelike motion.

Mike often adds a lead keel to the front hook bend to help get the fly down deeper and prevent it from flipping over. This added weight allows the Swinging D to maintain a more natural presentation in the water,

With the 2.0, original, and mini versions, Mike has a size for any condition.

imitating a wounded minnow with ease. The fly typically features a red collar of flash or feathers behind the foam head, which simulates gills and acts as a visual strike trigger for predators seeking an easy meal.

A standout design feature of this fly is the foam head, which is especially useful for fishing in smaller rivers where you often need to keep the fly forward of the boat. The head's buoyancy allows the fly to hover in the strike zone without needing constant stripping, maximizing your time in the water and enhancing the chances of a strike.

FISHING TECHNIQUES

The key to fishing the Swinging D successfully is varying your stripping speed. Dying baitfish are unpredictable, so don't rely on a robotic, uniform retrieve. Try fast strips with long pauses or slow strips with short pauses—mixing it up keeps the fly's movement erratic and lifelike. Smallmouth are notorious for striking during pauses, so don't be afraid to let the fly hang motionless in the water, or even allow it to hang for a beat before stripping it again. Often, the strike will come just as the fly is motionless or when it's moved slightly away from the fish.

Double Deceiver

(Originator and tier Mike Schmidt)

- **Hook:** B10s 1/0 and Ahrex Trout Predator sz 1
- **Thread:** Veevus 140 white
- **Keel weight:** .035 lead wire
- **Junction:** Senyo's Intruder Wire Large and Two 3d Beads - Yellow
- **Tail:** Barred Schlappen - Yellow
- **Rear Body:** Bucktail - Peach
- **Front Body:** Bucktail - Yellow, Brown, Peach
- **Eyes:** living eyes 8.5mm
- **UV cure:** RaidZap Thin

The Double Deceiver is a classic Deceiver pattern on steroids. Featuring a bucktail body and schlappen tail feathers, this fly creates a perfect baitfish profile that's sure to trigger aggressive responses from only the largest predatory fish in the system. At 6 inches, it strikes the ideal balance between size and action, and despite its size, it's incredibly easy to cast. Thanks to its narrow profile, it cuts through both water and air effortlessly, making it a joy to fish even in challenging conditions.

Bucktail is a hollow, natural material that produces a distinct, loud sound signature underwater. Each individual

This fly is a modern twist on the legendary Lefty's Deceiver—articulated and originally designed for chasing big brown trout. Its movement and profile make it just as effective for smallmouth, proving that good design crosses species lines.

strand of bucktail generates its own vibration, meaning there's no need for an added rattle to get the attention of fish. This fly can be tied in a variety of color combinations, but I've found that all-white, chartreuse and yellow, olive and white, and yellow and brown tend to be the most productive for me.

The Double Deceiver is designed to be fished on a sinking line to get it down into the strike zone. For smallmouth, I typically stick to an intermediate sinking line, but because of the fly's buoyant nature, it's often necessary to use a faster-sinking line, like a type 3 or 5, to ensure it gets down to where the fish are holding.

Another often overlooked feature of this fly is the lack of flash. Given its larger size and prominent profile, flash is unnecessary and could even work against you by being too intrusive. I love fishing this fly when the water is clearing up, and the fish are becoming more cautious and selective. The subtlety of the fly's presentation in these conditions often triggers strikes from wary fish. Plus, the large size of the fly itself draws attention from predatory fish looking for a big meal.

FISHING TECHNIQUES

When fishing the Double Deceiver, one rule I always stick to is: the larger the fly, the shorter the leader. A shorter leader allows for greater casting accuracy and helps avoid tangles. Let the fly settle and drift to one side, then give it a hard strip. Watch as the fly rights itself and starts swimming again. This dying action, like an injured baitfish, drives fish crazy, especially when the fly pauses or struggles in the water.

Big Bird

(Originator and tier Tony Sandrone)

What can I say? It's yellow and it works! Designed by Tony Sandrone of Nightmare Musky Flies, the Big Bird is an absolute killer bass bug that belongs in every angler's box. Super light and easy to cast, this fly moves with incredible action thanks to the halos of craft fur. It's built with two under collars of ¼-inch flex tubing that provide structure and a third collar for the head, adding to the fly's natural movement. Tied with just a rear hook and a front shank, the weight of the rear hook causes the fly to kick wildly in the water, creating an irresistible presentation.

I've said it before, and I'll keep saying it: smallmouth tend to eat larger streamers from the rear, so using a single hook doesn't hurt your hookup

The Big Bird has earned a spot in the boxes of many of my smallmouth fishing friends. It's not overly complicated to tie, which makes it accessible for tiers of all skill levels, but what really sets it apart is how it performs in the water. The materials give it excellent movement—just enough wiggle and flow to mimic a wounded baitfish.

rate—if anything, it makes it cleaner. The Lateral Scale flash and prominent eyes are major triggers for smallmouth, ensuring that this fly gets noticed in the water. Plus, it's neutrally buoyant, allowing you to fish it at whatever speed you prefer—fast or slow.

One common complaint I've heard from anglers is that craft fur and similar light-weight materials often foul up during a retrieve, messing with your presentation. I've found that with just one hook and the specific materials used in the Big Bird, this doesn't happen as often. The flex tubing helps separate and spread out the craft fur, allowing the fly to swim true. The large head design makes this fly dance under the surface, with the water hitting the head and pushing it side to side or up and down, just like a confused or wounded minnow. It's an all-around great fly that will serve you well in various fishing conditions.

FISHING TECHNIQUES

Fish the Big Bird on an intermediate or float-ing line, depending on your desired depth. Personally, I prefer to keep the fly moving steadily, pausing only briefly between strips. This approach gives it plenty of movement while also preventing the fish from having too much time to analyze it before commit-ting to the strike.

Drunk and Disorderly

(Originator and tier Tommy Lynch)

Tommy Lynch has truly nailed it with the Drunk and Disorderly, a fly that's a dead ringer not just for smallmouth, but also for trout and steelhead. This fly is a work of art, with its unique wedge-style head and overall construction that just flat-out works. Fished properly, it dips and dives all over the place, mimicking the erratic movements of a

- **Rear hook:** #2 Gamakatsu B10S
- **Thread:** Tan Danville 140 or 210
- **Tail:** Gold Holographic Flashabou
- **Body:** Gold Polar Chenille
- **Collar:** Natural variant rabbit Zonker
- **Wing:** Mallard flank
- **Connection:** 30 lb. wire
- **Beads:** 3D, natural color
- **Front hook:** #2/0 Gamakatsu 61413 jig
- **Finishing thread:** Kevlar or GSP 200, natural color
- **Tail:** Gold Holographic Flashabou
- **Body:** Gold Polar Chenille
- **Collar:** Natural variant rabbit Zonker
- **Front sides:** Mallard flank
- **Rattle:** Pyrex Rounded End Fly Rattle (3mm)
- **Front wing:** Gold Holographic Flashabou
- **Collar:** Natural variant rabbit Zonker
- **Head:** Deer body hair
- **Eyes:** 4mm earth 3D Living Eyes
- **Coating:** Solarez Thin or Ultra-Thin

The Drunk and Disorderly is a modern classic streamer, famous for its erratic, side-to-side action that triggers explosive strikes from big fish. Designed to be neutrally buoyant, it can be paused mid-retrieve, giving smallmouth the perfect window to commit.

distressed baitfish. The wedge head helps it dive through different water columns, triggering strikes from fish at various depths.

The Drunk and Disorderly is never sitting still. Its wedged head allows it to move constantly—whether it's chucking, diving, tipping, or howling (yes, howling!). Even at rest, the fly keeps moving because water flows over and around it, keeping its action alive during pauses. The internal flash in the front half of the fly, covered by mallard flank feathers, gives it a nearly fish-like appearance. Once wet, the flash bleeds through the feathers, creating a stunning effect similar to a Nuke Egg, making it appear almost translucent, adding to its lifelike appeal.

Because of its unique action and erratic movement, smallmouth don't just take this fly because it looks like a dying fish—they also hit it in territorial defense. The fly triggers a response: "Stay out of my space, this one's mine."

The Drunk and Disorderly has become a staple in my box. Tommy ties this fly in multiple sizes, ranging from a 2.5-inch to an 8-inch version, and I always make sure to carry a few of each size. The smaller ones are perfect for spring and early summer, especially when the water is low and clear. When the water's up and I'm fishing around structure, the larger sizes are a must.

In summary, the Drunk and Disorderly is a killer fly, and the time and thought that went into its design make it an essential tool in any angler's arsenal.

FISHING TECHNIQUES

This fly works best when you strip it while simultaneously guiding the rod tip. You need to actively direct the fly, as it's not a "set it and forget it" kind of pattern. Constantly work the fly back to the boat, adding pauses to keep the fish engaged. One strip, guide your rod tip to the left; the next, to the right; or maybe lift it slightly. These subtle, micro movements will travel down the line to the fly, giving it an erratic, lifelike action that's hard for fish to resist.

Tommy Lynch is a mastermind, offering sizes and colors for any condition and fish species.

- **Rear hook:** #2 Ahrex Trout Predator
- **Thread:** Fluorescent chartreuse Danville 140
- **Tail:** Barred tan over cream Stacked marabou
- **Tail flash:** Barred tan over cream Misfit Magnum Tinsel
- **Legs:** Sight Cast Marsh Legs, various colors
- **Body:** Tan Senyo's Super Satin Chenille
- **Collar:** Ginger hen saddle feathers
- **Mid-shank:** 15mm Chocklett Game Changer
- **Junction:** 20mm Chocklett Game Changer Shank, eye cut off
- **Front hook:** #1 Ahrex 26 Bent Streamer
- **Rattle:** Glass (3mm)
- **Weight:** Hareline Tungsten Shrimp Body (4mm)
- **Head:** Sand EP Crustaceous Brush (1.5")
- **UV glue:** RaidZap Flex

Woodsman

(Originator Mike Schultz; tied by Jake Villwock)

The Woodsman is a killer pattern designed by Mike Schultz up in Michigan. Drawing heavy inspiration from Russ Maddin's Circus Peanut, it's another purpose-built fly, crafted with the same precision and thoughtfulness as many of Mike's other creations. This fly was specifically designed to perform in colder waters, ranging from the mid-30s to mid-50s. When paired with an

The Woodsman is a blend of several flies, with its main purpose being to fish slowly in colder water temperatures around wood and heavy structure. Its design is made to stay in the strike zone longer, giving cold smallmouth plenty of time to react.

intermediate line and the right leader length, you can fish this fly incredibly slowly.

Its only weight comes from a tungsten jig back from Fulling Mill, though you could also use a Hareline Tungsten Shrimp Body. The body is grooved, allowing it to fit snugly around the hook shank. It is tied on top of the front hook, which allows it to ride hook up. This design provides weight without making the fly too heavy. This balance lets the fly hover, staying close to structure without sinking too quickly.

One unique feature that Mike built into this fly is what he calls a "tracer"—usually a set of white rubber legs or a lighter-colored head. Because the fly's natural colors can blend in with the water, it can sometimes be tough to track. The tracer makes it easier to spot the fly as it moves through the water.

The boys in Michigan really know how to design a fly—so much goes "under the hood." In this photo, you can see the finished fly alongside its components laid out.

In the colder months, typically from January to mid-March, fish tend to stay stationary in wood cover until they start moving around before the spawn. The name *Woodsman* reflects this characteristic, as it's designed to be cast into heavy wood cover, glide over logs, and hover in the zone without snagging too much.

Another strategic design element is the use of at least ten legs on each side. This is another one of Mike's tricks: even when the fly isn't moving, the legs add subtle motion. As Mike often says, "Fish aren't going to chase," so keeping a fly still can sometimes result in a lack of movement. With the legs, however, there's always some motion, creating a trigger even without physical movement.

Slow-moving is the name of the game with this fly. I've used it from late winter through early summer, and it works great when stripped—just be sure to give it a good pause in between strips.

FISHING TECHNIQUES

Fish the Woodsman slow—give it a solid strip and let it hover. Allow the rubber legs to undulate and move with the current. Being articulated twice, the fly will also have its own natural movement. Cast it close to structure, then slowly strip it back, varying the speed and rhythm of your strips. This technique will let the fly hover in place, giving those cold-water bass the chance to track it with confidence.

- **Rear hook:** #2 Ahrex Stinger
- **Shank:** 35mm Senyo's Intruder
- **Wire:** Large Senyo's Intruder Wire
- **Thread:** Olive Danville 140
- **Tail:** Bucktail
- **Flash:** Pearl Flashabou
- **Tail:** American rooster saddle
- **Overwing:** Peacock herl
- **Body:** Bucktail
- **Head:** Light olive EP Chromatic Brush
- **Eyes:** Bead chain

Flash Monkey

(Originator and tier Russ Maddin)

The Flash Monkey is another stellar streamer pattern from Russ Maddin, one of the pioneers of modern streamer design. Russ has been in the streamer game since the very beginning of articulated flies. He was part of the original crew of anglers who pushed the boundaries, going big and experimenting with articulation—and in doing so, he's developed some of the best streamers I've ever seen or fished. The first time I saw a Flash Monkey was while fishing with James Hughes out of Schultz Outfitters. After fishing it, I begged him to let me keep it, and I still have it to this day!

The Flash Monkey is a neutrally buoyant fly with minimal weight, coming mainly from the shank, hook, and bead-chain eyes. Russ wanted a fly that could be cast like a rocket but still retain

Another killer streamer from Russ Maddin, the Flash Monkey is a lightweight, easy-to-cast pattern. Its double bead-chain eyes add minimal weight while providing a solid profile and allowing the angler to fish it at any speed.

fish-like movement in the water. It's a lightweight and easy-to-throw streamer. The eyes are double bead chains, which don't add much weight but provide a solid profile. In its current version, Russ uses EP brushes for the head, creating bulk at the front of the fly. This bulk helps push water around the fly, creating hydraulic effects that assist in its movement.

The fly is designed to bend at a 90-degree angle when paused, mimicking the lifelike motion of a confused or stunned minnow. The original Flash Monkey is tied with a shank and a stinger hook, which helps keep fish hooked because it creates leverage during the fight. For larger waters and bigger fish, Russ also ties a tandem version. The larger version uses two Ahrex Trout Predator hooks and three beads to separate the hook gaps. When tying articulated flies, it's important to leave enough space between the hooks—otherwise, the fish may miss the fly due to a barrier effect created by the hooks being too close.

The Flash Monkey is an excellent baitfish pattern, not just for smallmouth, but also for trout. It was originally designed for Michigan trout but has made a significant impact in the warmwater world as well.

FISHING TECHNIQUES

Cast the fly toward the likely holding spot of your targeted fish, let it sit for a moment, then strip it hard once. Allow it to hover and bend with the water. Give it one or two small strips, then let it sit again. The key is to give the fly the action of a minnow that can't escape quickly—that's what drives predators crazy.

Circus Peanut

(Originator and tier Russ Maddin)

The Circus Peanut is a must-have fly in every angler's fly box. While it works for a variety of species, it truly shines when targeting smallmouth. In my opinion, Russ Maddin has created one of the best flies to ever hit the water. It has everything you need to trigger a strike—versatility, movement, and the perfect profile.

- **Rear hook:** #2 Ahrex Trout Predator
- **Thread:** Tan Danville 140
- **Tail:** Marabou, color of choice
- **Flash:** Flashabou, color of choice
- **Body:** Estaz (large), color of choice
- **Collar:** Hen saddle feathers
- **Front hook:** #2 Ahrex Trout Predator
- **Junction:** Large Senyo's Intruder Wire and 3D glass beads
- **Front collar:** Marabou, color of choice
- **Legs:** Barred Sili Legs, color of choice
- **Head:** Estaz (large), color of choice
- **Eyes:** Lead (medium)

The Circus Peanut is easily one of my go-to patterns for spring smallmouth, thanks to its natural color palette that excels in a variety of water conditions. When the water's dirty, I reach for black to increase visibility, and in clear water, I rely on olive to blend in with the natural forage. No matter the condition, it's a consistent producer.

The Circus Peanut brush head variant

The soft marabou tail provides constant movement, even when the fly is stalled, while the rubber legs are always in motion. Internal flash adds that extra shimmer, and the lead eyes help get the fly down into the strike zone quickly. The bulky head also pushes water, amplifying the fly's movement. I often add an accent color of chartreuse or orange, and just like with the Woodsman, I'll toss in a bit of white tracer for added visibility.

One of the Circus Peanut's standout features is its versatility in color combinations. I typically tie them in natural colors to match the bottom—olive over tan, tan and white, brown over tan, or even black and purple for those murky water days. The flash is subtle, with internal flash doing most of the work and just a few strands of Flashabou around the tail for extra attention. My personal favorite combo is tying the fly with double hooks and a shank off the back. This adds even more movement. The shank helps kick the tail around, and the extra joint gives the fly a more natural swimming

The Peanut is a confidence fly for me. In the spring, it's one of the first flies I tie on!

motion. The original design used two hooks and a few beads to separate them, but I prefer the added action of the shank.

You can adjust the weight of this fly by varying the size of the lead eyes, though I've found that medium lead eyes strike the perfect balance between weight and movement.

This fly is incredibly versatile, capable of mimicking a variety of prey, including crayfish, minnows, leeches, or even catfish. The key is matching the fly to the bottom you're fishing and keeping it close to structure. You want to keep it low in the water column, but not dragging along the bottom. Retrieve the fly until you feel it get hung up once or twice—then just speed up your retrieve slightly to keep it right in that sweet spot.

I find this fly especially effective in the early spring or when the water is colder. It sinks right into the zone, and the fish seem to go crazy for it. However, it's an all-season favorite of mine—use it in the summer, fall, and especially during the winter months when you're hunting for that one big fish.

FISHING TECHNIQUES

I like to fish the Circus Peanut by swimming it through deeper riffly water. Cast it slightly upstream and give it a mend to reduce tension on the fly, helping it sink more quickly. Mend every few seconds and pick up the slack, as the current provides plenty of tension on the fly. There's no need for aggressive stripping—just let the water do most of the work.

Another technique I enjoy is casting toward structure and then stripping the fly steadily back to the boat or shore. This allows the fly to move naturally in the current and triggers strikes from fish holding near the structure.

- **Hook:** #2 Ahrex Light Stinger
- **Thread:** White Danville 140
- **Tail:** Natural bucktail
- **Flash:** Pearl Flashabou
- **Collar:** White Ice Fur
- **Head:** Pearl Cactus Chenille (large)
- **Head tint:** Copic marker
- **Eyes:** 3D holographic

Murdich Minnow

(Originator Bill Murdich; tied by Todd Johnson)

Originally designed for striped bass, the Murdich Minnow continues to be a go-to fly for anglers targeting both freshwater and saltwater species around the globe. For me, it's a staple in my summertime smallmouth box. In the summer months, smallmouth have an abundance of food available, making it rare for them to chase baitfish. However, there are always those days when nothing else is working, and tossing a smaller, more natural baitfish pattern can be a game changer. The Murdich Minnow is the perfect size for those days. What I love about this fly is how easy it is to customize the color—you can change it up simply by using a marker on the top of the fly.

The Ice Wing shoulders of the Murdich Minnow give it a great platform for pushing water, adding subtle movement that mimics real baitfish. As a single-hook

A summer staple in my fly box, the Murdich Minnow is incredibly versatile, mimicking any baitfish, whether big or small. During the warmer months, I have the most success with smaller sizes, which seem to match the forage smallmouth are keying in on.

fly, it's easy to cast and work, making it an excellent option for anglers of all skill levels. I typically tie this fly on a size 2 hook, but it can easily be tied down to a size 8 or up to a 1/0 or larger, depending on the conditions and the species you're targeting. The Estaz head creates a nice translucent look in the water, making the fly even more lifelike.

I like to tie the Murdich Minnow in four color combinations: gray over white, chartreuse over white, tan over white, and olive over tan. I find these colors closely resemble the minnow species smallmouth typically feed on, making them incredibly versatile.

One of the best things about this fly is how easy it is to tie. With just five materials, it's less complicated and more affordable than some of the more intricate patterns out there. For anyone getting into the smallmouth game, this is an ideal fly to learn to tie.

Bass are ambush predators, so the more accurately you can present your streamer to structure, the better your chances. Since the Murdich Minnow is so easy to cast, it's also easier to present with precision. Keep it close to the structure you're fishing, and you're more likely to land a strike.

FISHING TECHNIQUES

With no added weight, the Murdich Minnow is great for fishing on a pause. What I love most about it for the summer months is that you can fish it slowly. Even when smallmouth are focused on other, more easily accessible food, a slowly presented baitfish can still trigger strikes. Try giving it short, slow strips with long pauses in between. This gives fish a chance to take notice of the fly and gives you the opportunity to pull it away from them, making it even more irresistible.

A natural variation of the Murdich Minnow

- **Rear hook:** #1/0 Gamakatsu B10S
- **Tail:** White schlappen feathers
- **Tail support:** Bucktail
- **Underbody:** Pearl UV Polar Chenille
- **Wing:** Bucktail
- **Collar:** Red Schlappen
- **Connection:** Intruder Trailer Hook with 3D bead
- **Front hook:** #2/0 Gamakatsu B10S
- **Flash:** Pearl Flashabou
- **Head:** Deer body hair

Sluggo

(Originator Chad Johnson; tied by Montana Fly Company)

The Sluggo was developed by Chad Johnson of Flippin, Arkansas, and initially designed for fishing the White and Norfolk Rivers. While it has earned a reputation for catching impressive brown trout, it has proven just as effective for smallmouth.

The fly was crafted with a big profile, yet it remains easy to cast. Most of it is built from bucktail, which is hollow and creates subtle vibrations as it moves through the water. Additionally, it doesn't absorb water, allowing the fly to shed water quickly during the cast. This unique feature makes it easy to throw and helps maintain its lively, active movement in the water. The spun deer

The Sluggo is a suspending swimbait with no added weight, making it versatile enough to be fished on a variety of fly lines with different sink rates. Its deer hair head pushes water, creating plenty of noise and movement underwater.

hair head creates a dying baitfish action that smallmouth find absolutely irresistible.

The UV Polar Chenille in the mid-body reduces the fly's overall weight, while adding a natural fish-like glow. To further enhance its lifelike appearance, adding a red collar of schlappen or additional Polar Chenille gives the fly even more realism.

The head of the fly floats, but when fighting against the sinking line, it creates a wobbling effect. The tail is free-swinging, so when the head stops, the tail follows naturally. When you pause the fly, it tends to roll over on itself—just like a rubber fluke or a wounded minnow. This movement drives smallmouth crazy.

Typically, I fish the Sluggo on an intermediate line for smallmouth, which allows you to stop it and let it hang for a few seconds before the line's sink rate catches up with the fly. I prefer a 7.5-foot leader, as it's short enough for easy casting but long enough to let the fly hang before sinking.

Every angler should have a few Sluggos in their box—they're simply too effective to overlook.

FISHING TECHNIQUES

With its spun deer hair head and bucktail body, the Sluggo is best fished with a sinking line. Start by giving it a couple strips or pops, then let it sit and wait for it to roll over on itself. When it does, strip again to create the erratic action smallmouth love. It's crucial to vary your stripping rhythm—this isn't the same as just stripping in to recast. For the fly to mimic a distressed baitfish, it needs to have lifelike, unpredictable movement.

BOTTOM BOUNCING

A handful of crayfish, ready for some summertime action

Subsurface fishing for smallmouth can sometimes feel like a mind-numbing task. It can be frustrating, especially when you lose a fly you spent thirty minutes tying, but it is an essential part of being productive when fishing for smallmouth. Bouncing flies along the bottom is what I consider the unsung hero of bass fishing. It's something that many anglers avoid—they'd rather get skunked throwing poppers or big baitfish patterns because those techniques are exciting. Watching a fish rise to eat a popper or seeing your streamer disappear as a fish inhales it—that's thrilling. But what happens when those techniques don't work?

The truth is, smallmouth are always eating, and they're constantly hunting just below the surface. Most ecosystems where smallmouth thrive are teeming with crayfish, stonecats, hellgrammites, leeches, and nymphs of all kinds. These are food sources that are consistently available to smallmouth. So why do so many anglers shy away from fishing them?

From experience, I can tell you that it's likely because subsurface fishing is the most effective yet the hardest way to fish for smallmouth. It's all about feel. Smallmouth are genetically built for short bursts of speed, and as I like to say, they close small gaps quickly. That means it's often difficult to feel when a smallmouth just pins your fly to the bottom. There's almost no tension in the line—it's just a subtle pause in your presentation. That pause can be tricky to detect, which is why many anglers struggle with it.

However, once you get the hang of subsurface fishing, I guarantee you'll fall in love with it. And fishing the bottom doesn't always mean targeting deep, dark holes. Smallmouth come into the shallows not only to eat bugs on the surface, but also to follow baitfish as they move up to warm up. Sight-fishing smallmouth as they track and pounce on a crayfish or stonecat imitation is incredibly rewarding and addicting.

A traditional crayfish designed by Dave Whitlock and tied by Allen Rupp, alongside a lifelike, fancy crayfish tied by Steve Silvario.

At the end of the day, subsurface fishing is a crucial component of smallmouth fishing. In this section, I'll highlight some of my favorite flies for fooling these fish at the bottom. We'll also dive into techniques, just like in the other sections, and I'll share some tricks I've picked up over the years to help you get hung up less when fishing the bottom.

Darters, camouflaged against the bottom, doing their best to stay hidden. But that's exactly what makes them such an easy, irresistible target for a hungry smallmouth.

Tied by Dave Troop, this little bug is incredibly effective when nothing else seems to work. He calls it the Coattail, but it's truly in a league of its own. Whether it looks like a worm, hellgrammite, or sculpin, it doesn't matter —fish eat it, and they eat it well.

Crawl Daddy

(Originator and tier Jake Villwock)

In the past, most crayfish patterns I encountered were tied with medium or large lead eyes. While getting a crayfish down to the bottom is crucial, I've found that too much weight can often be detrimental. Early in my guiding career, I spent more time and money tying crayfish patterns than I did actually fishing them. But after years of frustration, the conventional fishing world saw the

- **Hook:** #4 Ahrex Light Stinger
- **Thread:** Fluorescent chartreuse Danville 140
- **Shank:** 15mm Spawn 60 Degree Jig
- **Bead:** Olive Spawn Tungsten Football Bead (6mm)
- **Antennae:** Brown/black MFC Sexi Barred Legs (small)
- **Eyes:** Black EZ Shrimp Eyes (medium)
- **Hot spot:** Fluorescent orange EP Wooly Critter Brush
- **Under claws:** Brown Thin Fly Foam (3mm)
- **Claws:** Sculpin olive pine squirrel Zonker
- **Underbody:** Sculpin EP Tarantula Brush (1")
- **Overwing:** Rabbit Zonker fur
- **Legs:** Barred Sili Legs, color of choice
- **Collar:** Sculpin olive pine squirrel, spun in a dubbing loop

This is a fly I'm extremely excited to share, one that's been in the works for a few summers now. Designed to be smaller, lighter, and more natural in size, I wanted to create a pattern that could be fished on a floating line in both deep and shallow water. The Crawl Daddy is perfect for a slow retrieve, making it ideal for summertime smallmouth that are feeding more selectively.

introduction of a lure called the Ned rig—a small, 3-inch stick bait with air pockets at the tail to keep it upright. The moment it came out, every fly tier wanted to create a Ned fly because, well, the Ned worked—and it worked well.

However, my thought process was a little different.

I watched spin fishermen present these Ned rigs and quickly realized that, yes, the Ned looks like nothing yet everything at the same time—that's why it's so effective. But what intrigued me the most was the speed and control of the presentation. When you're fishing with 8-pound fluoro-carbon, there's not much surface area for the water to grab on to and pull the lure. So, my question was: how could we take the flies we have confidence in and present them in the same way?

I also observed my dad fishing unweighted rubber worms and noticed how many fish would strike before the worm even touched the bottom.

That's when I started designing a new fly. After several iterations, the Crawl Daddy was born. But creating the fly was just part of the process—the way we fished it had to change too. One of the first adjustments was in the sinking lines. We needed a method to control the speed and slow the cray-fish's descent. So, I started fishing all my

Smallmouth cruise the shallows all summer long, looking to ambush and pounce on crayfish.

subsurface flies on floating lines paired with a lighter fluorocarbon leader.

With that, the fly came together. I wanted a crayfish pattern that would sink slowly but also provide as much feel as possible on the bottom. The solution? Foam and tungsten. Together, tungsten gives you the best feel, while the foam balances the weight, allowing for better control. An unexpected benefit was that the back half of the fly stays slightly elevated off the bottom, reducing the chances of getting snagged. While you might still get stuck, most of the time it's just the head of the fly wedged in, so you can pull it free without much hassle.

Next, I focused on the profile. I wanted a nice taper to the body, but not too bulky, as that can affect both the sink rate and the action of the fly. For the underbody, I lightly wrapped EP Tarantula Brush, and for the shellback, I reverse-tied rabbit hair. This kept the fly light while still maintaining a great profile. Rubber legs were the next addition because smallmouth love them. I tie in three different colors to add to the mottled look, making it more lifelike. For the claws, I chose pine squirrel instead of rabbit, as our native crayfish tend to have smaller claws, making it easier for smallmouth to grab.

I could go on and on about the Crawl Daddy, but the bottom line is—it works. It holds up, doesn't snag as often, and is a must-have for low-water summer crayfishing.

FISHING TECHNIQUES

I recommend fishing the Crawl Daddy on a floating line with about a 10-foot leader. Cast slightly upstream and give it a good mend, but leave about 3 to 6 feet of fly line on the water. This will act as your indicator. Every so often, give it another mend and then pick up any slack. I almost never strip these flies, unless the boat is moving. Every time you mend, the fly pops up off the bottom and flutters back down, creating a natural, lifelike action. When the fly line stops, set the hook—an eat will often feel similar to bouncing over rocks, so it takes a little time to get used to. But once you do, I promise you'll love it.

Clawdad

(Originator Chuck Kraft; tied by Jake Villwock)

- **Hook:** #2 Ahrex Light Stinger
- **Thread:** Brown Danville 140
- **Claws:** Wood Eastern Trophies Clawdad Tails
- **Eyes:** Brown Sight Cast Hot Spot Lead Eyes
- **Body:** Dark olive/ginger variegated chenille (medium)
- **Legs:** Mud brown Wapsi Round Rubber Legs (medium)

We're back to the genius of Chuck Kraft for this one. The Clawdad was one of the first crayfish patterns I truly got excited about. It has everything you need—profile, movement, weight, and durability. Chuck was one of the first (if not *the* first) to stamp out his own claws from suede sheets. This innovative technique made the claws easy to tie on, helped them hold their profile, and made them incredibly durable. The bonus? When wet, the claws have a soft, rubbery feel that the fish seem to hold on to longer.

I spent a lot of time tying these flies when I first started using them. Because they were heavy, I lost quite a few, but I also caught a ton of fish. Over time, I started tying them with lighter lead eyes, and lo and behold, I started losing fewer

The Clawdad is one of the first crayfish flies I ever tied, and it quickly became one of my favorites. I tie them a bit lighter than the commercially available versions so I can fish them in skinny water during the summer, when smallmouth are prowling for crayfish.

flies. The Clawdad is an excellent fly—it's the closest thing I've seen to a conventional skirted jig. It's a rubber crayfish with a halo of rubber legs all around it. This type of bait is extremely popular among conventional smallmouth anglers, and for good reason. The legs move even when the fly is stationary underwater, which makes it very enticing.

The claws, originally created by Chuck, are now sold by William Heresniak of Eastern Trophies Fly Fishing. They come in a dozen colors, so you can match them with the right color chenille and round rubber legs. You can also mix and match colors to create any combination you want. Personally, I prefer the round rubber legs for this fly, although I've also tied them with Barred Sili Legs and they work just fine.

One of the things I really like about the original Clawdads are the solid painted eyes. I try to tie them as Chuck did, but honestly, I'm too lazy to paint my own eyes, so I buy the Sight Cast Fly Fishing painted lead eyes. The biggest size they offer is small, which is perfect for me—it keeps the fly light while still giving it that original look.

This fly has become one of my favorite summer patterns for smallmouth. It's not as intrusive as many other crayfish patterns, so when the water is low and clear, you can present the fly much closer to the smallmouth without spooking them. I typically fish these in a size 2 because they aren't bulky—they have a slender profile, allowing you to get away with using a slightly larger hook. A simple variant I like is dipping the tips of the claws in orange UV-curing glue. This adds a little trigger for the smallmouth, which seem to key in on that orange accent.

Now, let me emphasize something important. One thing you'll notice with all crayfish is that they all have orange somewhere on their bodies. The most common spot is the tips of their claws, but you'll also see it in the joints of their legs and sometimes even in the joints of their tails. This is crucial to note because I believe orange is a confidence color for smallmouth. It's a color they associate with food. So, in many of my bottom-crawling flies—whether they're crayfish or not—I always add a small hint of orange. It's something smallmouth key in on.

FISHING TECHNIQUES

The key to fishing the Clawdad is keeping it on the bottom, but out of the rocks. I fish most of my crayfish the same way—casting upstream with a floating line and mending as I float downstream. This technique allows the fly to stay in the zone longer than if you cast it at the bank and strip it back to the boat or your feet.

Another technique I've used in the past is fishing this fly under an indicator. Set the depth about 18 inches less than the water depth and let it float. You can pop the indicator from time to time to give the fly extra movement, which can help entice a strike.

Jiggy Craw

(Originator and tier Pat Cohen)

Pat Cohen not only is a master at stacking and sculpting deer hair for flies, but also excels when it comes to subsurface patterns. With a wealth of experience both fishing conventionally and fly fishing, Pat knows exactly what a fly needs to entice a strike. The Jiggy Craw is a perfect example of his expertise. As Pat himself explains, "The Jiggy Craw was created to imitate the standard crayfish bass jig that is regularly used by conventional anglers. No one can deny the success of such lures, so I needed a similar weapon in my fly-fishing arsenal."

- **Hook:** #2/0 Ahrex 26 Bent Streamer
- **Thread:** Olive Danville 210
- **Body:** Cohen's Crayfish Creature (medium)
- **Underbody:** Olive EP Tarantula Brush (1")
- **Antennae:** Brown/blue arctic fox
- **Eyes:** Black EP Crab Eyes
- **Weight:** Medium lead eyes and .030 lead-free wire
- **Ribbing:** Copper Ultra Wire (medium)
- **Rattle:** Glass (3mm)
- **Legs:** Olive/lt. olive/blue Hareline Fly Enhancer Legs

The Jiggy Craw might be a bit excessive for summer smallmouth, but when it comes to spring and winter, it's one of the first patterns I'll tie on. With its incredible movement, profile, and noise, it hits all the right triggers when the water is cooler, making it a go-to for lethargic fish.

Pat's insight is spot on—skirted jig-style lures are a staple in the conventional world, and their success speaks for itself. As we discussed earlier with Chuck Kraft's Clawdad, the rubber leg skirts are key to adding movement to a fly when presented slowly along the bottom. But the Jiggy Craw goes far beyond that.

Pat has strategically incorporated a rattle in the fly's underbody and placed it on top of the lead eyes. Additionally, he adds non-lead wire directly behind the eyes to further weight the front of the fly. This design works exceptionally well with a jig hook, helping the hook eye stay pointed up and allowing the fly to slide over rocks with ease.

Another critical component of the Jiggy Craw is the underbody, which uses EP Tarantula Brush. This is a material I often use in my own flies because of its versatility. It's a semi-dense brush that can be palmered loosely for a less dense underbody or tightly packed and sculpted to any shape or profile. The EP Tarantula Brush is also paired with small rubber legs that create additional movement, especially when the fly is slowly dragged along the bottom. The material comes in a variety of colors, offering options for any situation. Its wire core adds durability, and while it may require heavy-duty scissors or small wire cutters to cut, the wire ensures that the brush material

The Jiggy Craw is a killer wintertime smallmouth fly.

can protect a glass rattle from breaking—something you don't often get with other materials wrapped around rattles.

A true standout of the Jiggy Craw is the Cohen's Crayfish Creature body. These bodies come in a standard white, allowing the tier to color, paint, or dye them to their preference. Pat is a true artist when it comes to dyeing, often using clothing dye to dip the claws in one color and the rest of the body in another. He then adds further accents

Crayfish are abundant and come in all sizes and colors. I've found that olive with hints of blue, tan, or orange tend to work best for me.

with markers or by splattering the body with additional dyes.

I often tie Jiggy Craws for winter and spring fishing, as I find they work great with the legs, weight, and rattle when trying to get cold smallmouth to bite. That said, I'll also buy them from Pat for his incredible craftsmanship—his work on the bodies is simply amazing.

For those looking for a smaller version of the fly, Pat's Sweet Baby Cray is a perfect option. This fly mimics smaller crayfish, particularly useful during low summer flows or late in the summer when the baby crays are more prevalent. It doesn't feature rubber legs, making it a great choice for those situations.

FISHING TECHNIQUES

The Jiggy Craw excels when fishing structure. Pat recommends, "After casting to rocky structure, I use my rod tip to give the fly two to five little twitches, then let it settle back to the bottom. The rubber legs move in the current and umbrella out on the drop." These twitches not only add action to the fly, but also activate the rattle, giving smallmouth something else to home in on.

When fishing in the spring, I prefer to use a floating line, casting upstream, letting the fly sink, and stripping it back while keeping the slack tight. I also add periodic lifts to get the fly off the bottom and keep the action going.

- **Thread:** Fluorescent orange Veevus 140
- **Rear shank:** 20mm Flymen articulated shank
- **Legs:** Eight strands medium Sexi-Floss, color of choice
- **Antennae:** Two or four strands of medium red Sexi-Floss
- **Bump:** RD Frenzy Fly Brush (1"), color of choice
- **Claws:** Pine squirrel Zonker, color of choice
- **Eyes:** Mono Eyes, color of choice
- **Body:** RD Lively Leg Brush (1"), color of choice
- **Carapace:** Olive mallard flank feather
- **Resin:** RaidZap Flex
- **Connection:** 20mm shank
- **Front hook:** #1/0 Ahrex 26 Degree Down Eye
- **Keel:** .030 lead wire
- **Bump:** RD Frenzy Fly Brush (1"), color of choice
- **Rattle:** Glass (5mm)

- **Body:** RD Lively Leg Brush (1"), color of choice
- **Carapace:** Olive mallard flank
- **Legs:** Six or eight Sili Legs, color of choice, tied in on either side of fly
- **Throat:** Flesh barred rabbit Zonker
- **Head:** Backcountry EP Crustaceous Brush

Fleein' Cray

(Originator and tier James Hughes)

I'm going to start by saying that, technically, this fly is not a bottom-bouncing pattern. It is a swim fly, but we're placing it in the bottom category because it's a crayfish imitation. However, the Fleein' Cray is unique and one of a kind, designed by the mastermind James Hughes of Schultz Outfitters. The rivers and river structures in Michigan are quite different from many of the rivers

A hybrid crayfish, the Fleein' Cray isn't designed to be fished on the bottom but rather like a swim fly. Strip it hard and let it sit, mimicking a crayfish trying to escape quickly. Created by James Hughes from Michigan, this fly has taken the bass world by storm with its lifelike action and effectiveness.

Changer Craw
- **Hook:** #2 Ahrex Minnow
- **Thread:** Danville 140, color of choice
- **Claws:** Tan barred rabbit Zonker
- **Claws and carapace:** Tan Chocklett Factory Craw Claws Carapace (medium)
- **Antennae:** Black Spanflex
- **Legs:** Pumpkin / green / red flake Barred Sili Legs
- **Underbody:** Tan Chocklett's Filler Flash
- **Body:** Tan grizzly hen saddle
- **Eyes:** Lead (medium)
- **Shanks:** 10mm Chocklett Game Changer

Changer Hellgrammite
- **Hook:** #2 Ahrex Minnow
- **Thread:** Black Veevus 6/0
- **Tail/legs:** Black Spanflex
- **Underbody:** Black Blane Chocklett Finesse Brush (5")
- **Shellback:** Black Chocklett Factory Hellgrammite Body Part
- **Shanks:** 10mm Chocklett Game Changer
- **Eyes:** Lead (medium)

Changer Craw and Hellgrammite

(Originator and tier Blane Chocklett)

The **Changer Craw** is yet another brilliant creation from Blane Chocklett. When he first introduced the Game Changer platform years ago, it's hard to imagine anyone could have predicted just how versatile it would become. From dry flies to nymphs and everything in between, this platform brings an incredible lifelike movement to any fly pattern.

The Changer Craw has quickly become one of my favorite flies to use during the summer months. With Blane's new foam claws and carapace kits, you can tie this fly in sizes ranging from 5 inches down to 2 inches, allowing you to tailor it to any situation or target species. The foam helps elevate the back of the fly off the bottom, giving it a dynamic, fighting

The Changer Craw (left) and Hellgrammite (right) are two of my favorite flies to tie and fish for smallmouth—the realistic movement is absolutely insane. It's always a bummer to lose one, and I've definitely been known to go swimming after them, but there's nothing quite like the thrill of fishing with these patterns.

crayfish action. The hen feathers used for the body, paired with the shanks, create an unmatched movement that truly mimics a crayfish in distress.

One of Blane's signature techniques is smashing the lead eyes flat, which serves a dual purpose: it helps the fly stay on the bottom longer by allowing it to slide more easily over rocks, and the flattened lead provides a bit of resistance as the fly falls, which slows the descent, making it even more realistic in its movement. While the Changer Craw can be tied in a variety of colors, I've found that natural colors work best, with olive being my top producer.

The **Changer Hellgrammite** is another incredible fly designed by Blane. I hadn't tied one until he released the new foam shellback kits, and now that they're available, I'm hooked. The original pattern

Black is another great color for a hellgrammite.

required UV glue or other materials to create the shellback, which felt like a bit too much work for me. But now, with these kits, I've tied a few, and they swim beautifully.

What I love about the Changer Hellgrammite is its versatility. While it's a bottom-bouncing nymph, it can also double as a small swim fly. If you look at the lead on this fly, you'll notice it's flattened in the same way Blane does with his crayfish. This gives the fly an excellent swimming motion in the water. The foam not only helps counterbalance the lead, but also allows the fly to fall slower and ride higher off the bottom. Hellgrammites are larger nymphs that thrive in well-oxygenated water, and when disturbed, they "swim" back down to the rocks. This fly captures that natural behavior perfectly.

The Changer Craw and Hellgrammite might take a little extra time to tie, and as a guide, it's always tough when a client says, "Oops, I broke it off." But when they hold up, they are absolutely worth every minute spent at the vise. The action of these flies is unmatched in the fly-fishing world right now—and I'd argue that it's unparalleled in the fishing industry as a whole.

The Changer Craw is a deadly bottom-bouncer —it's got the profile, movement, and realism that smallmouth can't resist. Bounce it along the rocks and get ready—because they go crazy for it.

So, call up your local fly shop and order your components today—you won't regret it when you see how these flies perform!

FISHING TECHNIQUES

For the Changer Craw, I like to fish it similarly to a swim fly, but I keep it close to the bottom. I'll cast it to my targeted spot, let it sink, then strip it slowly, giving it a little pop at the end of each strip. The pop lifts the fly off the bottom, so during the pause, the fly is falling naturally without getting caught on rocks.

For the Changer Hellgrammite, I fish it more like a traditional crayfish or larger nymph. I cast it slightly upstream, let it sink, then give it a mend to remove slack. I repeat this process throughout the drift. Another technique I use is fishing it under an indicator in faster, deeper water. This allows me to keep the fly in the strike zone while using the indicator to detect any strikes.

- **Hook:** #2/0 Ahrex 26 Bent Streamer
- **Thread:** Brown UTC 140
- **Eyes:** Red/white/black Hareline Double Pupil Lead Eyes (XL)
- **Extra weight:** Tungsten bead (5/32")
- **Hot spot:** Orange rabbit Zonker
- **Claws:** Natural tan rabbit Zonker
- **Shellback:** Brown/orange Hareline Crazy Legs
- **Body:** Natural tan rabbit Zonker
- **Collar:** Tan hen saddle
- **Head:** Natural tan rabbit Zonker, spun in a dubbing loop

Single Fly Cray

(Originator and tier Mike Schultz)

The final crayfish pattern for this section is one that has become a staple in fly boxes across the Midwest, the Single Fly Cray by Mike Schultz. It's an absolute killer in the early season when water temperatures are on the colder side. Mike specifically ties this version with XL lead eyes, which help it sink quickly and stay on the bottom during winter and early spring fishing. The fly is primarily constructed from rabbit Zonker and hen saddle, giving it natural, lifelike movement—perfect for when you're fishing slowly along the bottom.

What really stands out about Mike's design is the mottled look he's achieved

From the mind of Mike Schultz, this fly has the perfect combination of movement and profile. Mike loves fishing the Single Fly Cray in the early spring and late winter, when the fish are more sluggish and need something that really stands out.

by blending materials in a way that mimics the natural color transitions in crayfish. The darker browns and oranges bleed through the tan base, creating that realistic appearance.

Many of the rivers Mike fishes in the Midwest have sandy bottoms, so the crayfish tend to be on the lighter side. For other regions, I'd suggest tying this fly in olive or brown to better match the riverbed. As Russ Maddin wisely puts it, if you're trying to imitate a specific prey item, keep your fly as close as possible to the color of the river bottom. Crayfish, and other bottom-dwelling creatures, instinctively try to blend in, so a natural color scheme will make your fly less conspicuous and more likely to entice a predator.

Another thoughtful touch is how Mike has added rubber legs to enhance the fly's movement. The antennae and the light skirt of legs around the head are perfectly balanced—not too much, not too little. This strategic addition helps the fly behave even more like a live crayfish.

Over the years, I've spent a lot of time experimenting with this fly, tying it just like Mike's original design, especially when I'm targeting colder waters. However, I've also downsized it on occasion, using medium or small lead eyes. With lighter eyes, the fly's fall is slower, giving the fish more time to observe it as it sinks. I've found that with many subsurface patterns, lighter flies that fall more slowly tend to get more strikes as they hit the bottom. The key is that the fish can see it fall—mimicking the natural motion of a crayfish that's been spooked from a rock. When they flee, they whip their tails and shoot backward, then eventually fall back to the bottom to seek shelter. While a slower sink might take more time, it gives you the advantage of fishing as soon as the fly hits the water.

FISHING TECHNIQUES

Fish it low and slow. The Single Fly Cray is designed to stay on the bottom, so focus on keeping it there. You can let it sit a moment, then slowly strip it back to the boat. If you're wading, cast slightly upstream and retrieve the fly back to you with a slow, steady strip. The goal is to make the fly behave like a crayfish casually moving along the riverbed, tempting predators into striking.

S3 Sculpin

(Originator and tier Mike Schultz)

The S3 Sculpin has been a staple in many smallmouth anglers' fly boxes for nearly a decade now. I can still remember watching Mike Schultz tie this fly when I was living above the shop and managing one of the TCO Fly Shop locations more than ten years ago. I've definitely put this fly to the test myself, and I can confidently say it's a winner.

- **Hook:** #2/0 Ahrex 26 Bent Streamer
- **Thread:** Black UTC 140
- **Eyes:** Black/orange/black Hareline Double Pupil Lead Eyes (large)
- **Extra weight:** Tungsten bead ($5/32$")
- **Tail:** Olive barred rabbit Zonker
- **Body:** Olive barred rabbit Zonker
- **Body:** Tan barred rabbit Zonker
- **Collar:** Olive hen saddle
- **Legs:** Olive Barred Sili Legs
- **Pec fins:** Olive barred rabbit Zonker and strung marabou
- **Flash:** Red/copper Flashabou
- **Head:** Dark olive rabbit Zonker
- **Wings:** Ginger badger rooster saddle feather

Another gem from Mike Schultz, this fly has an excellent sculpin profile. I've been fishing the S3 Sculpin for over ten years and have no plans of stopping anytime soon—it's been a consistent producer and a staple in my fly box.

Sculpins are an important part of the smallmouth's diet, but here's an interesting fact: they're not tolerant of warm water. Because of this, many of our warmwater fisheries don't have sculpins. However, smallmouth migrate into smaller, cooler creeks to spawn in the spring, and these creeks often contain sculpins. The young smallmouth that grow up in these creeks quickly learn that sculpins are a great food source. That said, whether sculpins are present or not, smallmouth are opportunistic predators—they will strike at anything that resembles food.

Another fun tidbit about sculpins is that they resemble darters, which are abundant in most warmwater fisheries. So, regardless of whether sculpins are present, this fly will still look like something a smallmouth should eat, making it an essential pattern to fish.

Mike's design of the S3 Sculpin is topnotch. The fly holds its profile well when wet, and each wrap of material adds bulk and definition. With rabbit fur making up the tail and much of the body, you get a nice taper down to a point, which perfectly mimics the shape of many bottom-dwelling prey items that smallmouth are accustomed to eating. The small amount of flash on top adds just the right touch of movement and glitz to catch the attention of smallmouth, especially when fished with subtle strips.

What I really love about the S3 Sculpin is that the only fluorescent color on the fly is the orange eyes, one of my favorite trigger colors for smallmouth. The lack of excessive flash or fluorescent color means it can be fished in various water conditions without worrying about spooking fish with too much flash or color.

Olive is always my go-to color when it comes to matching natural tones. It seems to blend well with just about any river bottom color. That said, I also like tying this fly in lighter color combinations, such as brown and tan, tan and sand, or light olive and tan. On the flip side, when the water is dirty, I make sure to have a few black and purple versions on hand. The darker colors really help smallmouth locate the fly when visibility is low.

FISHING TECHNIQUES

I personally prefer to swim this fly, even though it's tied with lead eyes and is designed to stay low and slow. I like to keep it moving with a decent pause now and then. Unlike minnows, sculpins and many bottom-dwelling creatures don't swim in a typical, steady pattern. They scurry along the bottom, darting in short bursts, which is exactly the kind of motion you want to replicate with the S3 Sculpin.

Freeze Dried Sculpin

(Originator and tier Jake Villwock)

Named after the meals you eat while backpacking, the Freeze Dried Sculpin is a must-have snack for smallmouth. Though it has "Sculpin" in its name, the profile of this fly could easily resemble that of a baby hog-nose sucker, stonecat, or darter. So, yes, it's a sculpin, but it can effectively imitate a wide variety of food sources for smallmouth. The key is presenting it on the bottom, allowing it to

- **Rear shank:** 25mm Chocklett Game Changer
- **Hook:** #2 Ahrex Light Stinger
- **Thread:** Brown Danville 140
- **Tail:** Ginger mallard flank
- **Underbody:** Copper UV Polar Chenille
- **Collar:** Sand EP Tarantula Brush (1")
- **Overwing:** Brown arctic fox fur
- **Junction:** Large Senyo's Intruder Wire with 3D bead
- **Eyes:** Yellow/white/black Hareline Double Pupil Lead Eyes (medium)
- **Pec fins:** Brown Barred Sexy Floss
- **Head:** Dark brown/natural deer body hair

The Freeze Dried Sculpin is one of the first slider-style flies I ever tied, and it's super fun to create. It has a fantastic profile in the water, and the medium lead eyes are counterbalanced by the deer hair, helping it glide smoothly and reducing the chances of getting stuck.

scurry around like many of the natural prey smallmouth are used to.

The Freeze Dried Sculpin was a fly I became obsessed with for a long time, and it gave me the perfect excuse to keep experimenting with slider-style heads. Typically, I tie them in two color combinations, olive/brown and tan/brown, but I've also tied them in black/purple, white/red, and orange/tan. Truthfully, the color combinations are endless, but I tend to keep them on the natural side. The black/purple version is especially effective when the water is dirty, making it harder for smallmouth to pick up on the silhouette of the more natural-colored patterns.

I've found that this fly really shines for me in the colder months; some of my best winter days have been spent fishing it. It sinks quickly, and the flash, combined with the

When the water's dirty, a black Freeze Dried Sculpin is never a bad choice. The dark profile stands out in low visibility and gives fish a clear target—perfect for getting noticed when conditions are tough.

hot-colored eyes, really makes it stand out. I don't fish it much in low, clear water in its current form, but with Greg Senyo's new Super Satin Polar Chenille coming out, I'm eager to tie a few with that. I'll swap out the medium lead eyes for small ones, which will help keep the profile I want while removing most of the flash. This will also make the fly lighter, allowing me to fish it effectively in the lower summer flows.

When I was experimenting with the deer hair slider design, I was careful not to bulk up the body of the fly too much. Deer hair is naturally buoyant, and even with lead eyes, it can significantly slow the sink rate. I wanted the fly to have a solid profile without the added weight and bulk of dense materials. Like many of today's trout nymphs, I believe less is more. I wanted a fly that would drop quickly and that I could feel well when it bounced off rocks or got softly pegged to the bottom by a smallmouth.

After a few renditions, I settled on a mix of mallard flank, UV Palmer Chenille, EP Tarantula Brush, and a light amount of arctic fox fur to create the profile I was after. These materials are all relatively light and not very bulky when proportioned properly as you tie them on. The rubber legs for pectoral fins add movement, and when viewed from above, they also help maintain the fly's overall tapered profile. The mallard flank is a fantastic material for adding dimension to a fly; its naturally barred appearance contributes to the fly's realism, mimicking the subtle patterns found in nature.

This fly is tied with just one hook and a rear shank. I chose this design because the overall length of the fly places the hook right in the middle. Since there isn't a lot of material to fight through, fish don't seem to have any issues getting hooked. It also makes it easier to remove the hook if the angler is a little late on the hook set.

FISHING TECHNIQUES

I prefer to keep this fly on the bottom, fishing it low and slow. One of the great features of the slider head is that the deer hair acts as a semi–weed guard, reducing the chances of it getting snagged. During the winter months, I typically fish the Freeze Dried Sculpin with a floating line and a fluorocarbon leader. This setup allows me to control the speed of the presentation without worrying about a sinking line and fast current pulling the fly out of the zone too quickly. The key is to fish it low and slow—just make it scurry and bounce along the bottom.

Womp Rat

(Originator and tier Jake Villwock)

The Womp Rat is the big brother to the Freeze Dried Sculpin, and it came about in a bit of an unexpected way. I was tying what I used to call the "Freeze Dried XL Sculpin," and as I got to the head, I realized I was out of razor blades to trim the deer hair. So, I grabbed some Tarantula Brush, palmered it on, and trimmed the bottom to give it a slider shape. I stared at it for a while and couldn't help but like the way it looked

The Womp Rat is new to my arsenal this year, but it's already proven itself time and time again. This fly can be fished on the bottom, as a swim fly, or swung through slower riffles. It's a buggy pattern that imitates a variety of smallmouth forage, making it incredibly versatile in different conditions.

better than the deer hair head. I quickly realized that the Tarantula Brush made for a bulkier head, wider in some areas and narrower in others, which gave it the perfect shape to resemble a sculpin.

Once that light bulb went on, I decided to tweak a few things. I reduced the density of the fly by using less material overall. I wanted it to hold a profile, but I also wanted the entire fly to move naturally—whether being actively retrieved or just sitting on the bottom. The goal was to create that classic sculpin mottling, with a little hidden flash mixed in. I also added a rattle for some extra noise when conditions called for it.

I experimented with a couple of new materials from Montana Fly Company and Greg Senyo. His Dirty Bird Dubbing works perfectly to cover the junctions between the hooks and shanks, and because it's a longer-fibered dubbing, you can tie it in neatly. I also tried his Super Satin Chenille, which isn't flashy, but it fills in the underbody nicely without drawing too much attention.

The final tweak was in how I connected the two hooks. Instead of using wire and a bead like I usually do, I decided to try the method Mike Schultz uses on all his flies—connecting them with a shank. To give myself a little extra space between the hooks, I threaded a bead onto the shank and tied it in. It worked! After fishing it a few times, it didn't take long for the Womp Rat to become a go-to in my fly box. One thing I really like about it is that the hooks ride up, which allows you to crawl the fly

In cooler temps, the Womp Rat excels. Fish it low and slow; the inverted hooks make it easier to crawl over rocks.

along the bottom or over logs with more confidence that it won't get snagged as easily—certainly less than with two hooks facing downward.

I'd say this fly is the perfect combination of the Freeze Dried Sculpin and Russ Maddin's Circus Peanut.

Sculpins are a must-have for smallmouth, not necessarily because they eat them all the time, but because sculpins are an easy, opportunistic meal. Smallmouth love baby catfish, stonecats, and madtoms—all of which have a similar profile to a sculpin. After years of having success with sculpin patterns, I realized that while they might not be in all of our systems, stonecats are abundant, and smallmouth go crazy for them.

Honestly, I'm convinced smallmouth don't know the difference, and frankly, it doesn't matter—they eat sculpin flies because they resemble those smaller catfish.

FISHING TECHNIQUES

The Womp Rat is a hybrid fly, which makes it versatile. It can be fished low and slow along the bottom, but it can also be fished as a swim fly in the mid-column. If I'm fishing it on the bottom, I'll slowly pull it along, occasionally giving it a pop here and there to add some movement. If I'm fishing it as a swim fly, I'll use a floating or intermediate line so I can strip it and pause it without the fly and line sinking too quickly.

Smoke N Mirrors Sculpin

(Originator and tier Dan Melrose)

- **Hook:** #2 Owner 60 Jig
- **Thread:** Red Danville 140
- **Shank:** Dirty Water Tail Feather Spine
- **Eyes:** Dirty Dumbbell Eyes (3/16")
- **Tail:** Olive marabou
- **Flash:** Opal Lateral Scale
- **Body:** Copper Polar Chenille
- **Hot spot:** Red UV Ice Dub
- **Overwing:** Orange bucktail
- **Collar:** Olive Marabou
- **Pec fins:** Orange Larva Lace Barred Round Rubber Legs

Designed by Dan Melrose of Dirty Water Fly Company, I remember purchasing some Smoke N Mirrors about fifteen years ago on a recommendation from a friend. He said, "If you want some killer streamers, call Dan," so I did. Initially designed for trout, that's what we fished for with them, and I can honestly say I had never experienced such a day of streamer fishing until I lost the only black one I had. After that, they sat in my "trout streamer" box for a couple of years, but out of necessity and a lack of time to tie, I pulled them out before a smallmouth float. I had olive and white ones, and after about a week of fishing them, they were nearly chewed up, so I had to start tying them myself!

The Smoke N Mirrors is a fantastic sculpin fly with all the right triggers to entice smallmouth. Its profile, movement, and presentation are perfect for mimicking the forage smallmouth are keying in on.

Dan makes his own shanks out of lighter-gauge wire, and I think they work great. The light, wispy marabou tail and the minimal materials on the tail really give this fly a realistic swimming motion. The orange accent color in the bucktail and the rubber legs add even more versatility—this fly can imitate a sculpin, a crayfish, or any other tasty morsel a smallmouth might fancy. The brass eyes with the tungsten conehead provide the perfect amount of weight and create the ideal wide-to-pointy head profile of so many baitfish. It's really a smoke-and-mirrors fly—it looks like everything but doesn't quite look like anything.

Dan is a streamer nut, and his flies are designed with precision—everything on this fly serves a purpose. Even the small red UV Ice Dub collar on the head and midsection might not look like much to us, but fish can see UV colors better than we can. It's another trigger that makes this fly so effective. He thought of everything with this one, which is why I always have a good number of these in my box year-round.

Like the Freeze Dried Sculpin, I plan to experiment with Senyo's Super Satin Polar Chenille for this fly as well, to reduce the flashiness for low summer flows. The Smoke N Mirrors really shines when the water has a greenish hue or when it's slightly high but still relatively clear.

This particular one is tied on a size 2 Owner Jig Hook, with an overall length of 2.5 inches, but you can also tie them on size 1, 1/0, or larger hooks for a bigger profile. I find the smaller ones work best in the summer months, but in the winter and spring, I prefer the larger ones—more for the fish to wrap their mouths around.

Fun fact about sculpins: they love to eat fish eggs. So, in the spring, when smallmouth are migrating to spawn and are in what I call the "clean out" stage—basically, when they're trying to remove all predators from their surroundings—the sculpin fly becomes incredibly effective.

FISHING TECHNIQUES

I like to fish this fly like a swim fly but slower, giving it constant action with longer pauses. Because the Smoke N Mirrors has a relatively aggressive angle on the jig hook, it's harder to get stuck on rocks. When you strip it, it tends to slide up and over any subsurface structure. It's a great fly for when the water is colder but you still want a fly that's moving.

Stoned Cat

(Originator and tier Jake Villwock)

- **Hook:** #2 Ahrex Light Stinger
- **Shank:** 10mm Chocklett Game Changer
- **Junction:** Large Senyo's Intruder Wire
- **Beads:** Tungsten ($5/32"$)
- **Tail/overwing:** Brown barred rabbit Zonker
- **Underbody:** Tan EP Wooly Critter Brush
- **Collar:** Brown rooster saddle feather
- **Pec fins:** Brown MFC Barred Sexi-Floss (medium)
- **Whiskers:** Brown MFC Barred Sexi-Floss (small)
- **Head:** Tan EP Foxy Brush, colored to match rabbit

For many who don't know, the stonecat, or madtom, is a small catfish that lives under rocks in many smallmouth rivers. It's a staple in the diet of smallmouth bass, and many bait fishermen will tell you that it's the only thing you need to catch them. They say it's like ice cream on a hot day in the summer to these fish!

So, why aren't there more patterns out there that mimic these fish? Well, in some ways, there are plenty. Sculpin patterns can double as small catfish—they share a similar profile. But I couldn't leave well enough alone, so I decided it was time to create an actual stonecat pattern.

The Stoned Cat is a creation of mine designed to fill a gap in the fly world. The stonecat, or madtom, is a small catfish species that smallmouth absolutely love to eat. This fly perfectly mimics that elusive forage.

The Stoned Cat is a single articulated fly that's designed to replicate the stonecat's profile. It starts with a small, 10mm tail shank and a tan Wooly Critter Brush underbody. For the tail, I use a trimmed and tapered rabbit Zonker strip. The body portion of the fly is where things get interesting and, in my opinion, what makes this fly stand out.

The underbody is made with the same Wooly Critter Brush, palmered in the usual manner, but the top is where the real magic happens. I cut rabbit fur off the hide and reverse-tie it to get a nice, tapered body. I spread the hair across the entire top of the fly, which widens the profile. I repeat this process twice, adding a small collar of rooster saddle feathers for structure and shape.

The pec fins are made with medium-size Barred Sexi-Floss, and I use the same but in small for the whiskers. The head is made from EP Fox Brush, palmered and trimmed off the bottom. After that, I use Copic markers to color the head to match the color of the rabbit fur.

The bottom view of the fly shows the angler what really makes the Stoned Cat stand out, the tungsten beads strategically placed in the rear of the hook.

One design feature I borrowed from the Fly Fish Food guys is the use of tungsten beads in place of traditional lead eyes. I tie in two tungsten beads "belly-scratcher" style, but with one twist. Instead of placing the beads along the entire length of the fly, I position them toward the back third of the hook shank. This unique placement allows the fly to drop horizontally in the water column, but it also keeps the center of the fly the lowest when on the bottom. This helps the hook eye point upward, allowing the fly to skate over rocks rather than dig beneath them.

All of these design features, while they might seem simple, are placed on the fly for a reason. I use the shank for the tail to add more movement when the fly is fished. It also creates a hinge point that allows the tungsten beads to pull the middle of the fly down, keeping the hook point up and preventing it from snagging.

The Stoned Cat has quickly become a staple in my box and was recently picked up by Montana Fly Company. It, along with many of my smallmouth flies, is set to launch in 2026.

FISHING TECHNIQUES

The Stoned Cat is another fly I fish on a floating line with a fluorocarbon leader. I want this little dude to stay low in the water and just tumble across and around the rocks. You can swing it through riffles too, but I find the slower you can present this fly, the better. Take the same techniques I use for my Crawl Daddy crayfish and apply it to this one.

Crittermite

(Originator Chuck Kraft; tied by Jake Villwock)

- **Hook:** #4 Ahrex Traditional Shrimp
- **Thread:** Olive brown Danville 140
- **Body:** Olive CK Crittermite Tail
- **Head:** Olive CK Game Changer Tail
- **Underbody:** Sculpin EP Wooly Critter Brush
- **Legs:** Mud brown Wapsi Round Rubber Legs (medium)
- **Pincher:** Brown Barred Centipede Legs
- **Eyes:** Olive Sight Cast Hot Spot Lead Eyes (small)

The Crittermite is another master-piece from the mind of Chuck Kraft. I have been fishing this fly for about fif-teen years now, and it never seems to disappoint.

When I first started fly fishing for smallmouth, I had heard of these bugs called hellgrammites, the nymph stage of the dobsonfly—an equally scary-looking bug. But smallmouth love them. I tied many of the OG hellgrammite flies and even messed around with some of my own designs, but when Chuck first showed me this at the Somerset Fly Fish-ing Show, my first response was, *Where and when can I get those bodies?* A week later, I got a package in the mail, and the rest is history. I've messed around with different ways to tie them—six legs, four legs, articulated, heavy, light, different underbody materials—but the

The Crittermite is a fly I'll always have in my box. Whether fished as a streamer, nymph, or under an indicator, it's incredibly versatile. No matter how you present it, smallmouth seem to have it in their DNA to eat this fly.

fly displayed will forever be the winning combination!

The hellgrammite is a bug you can find in small cracks and crevices along most river bottoms. They can be found under rocks or clinging onto wood or even lost anchors and fishing rods in the river. The pinchers on these things can draw blood, yet for some reason, smallmouth absolutely love them. Maybe it's their size—they can grow up to 4 inches long—or maybe it's just the sheer number of them in the river. Either way, it's a fly I never leave the ramp without.

Chuck's bugs are made of the same suede material that his Clawdad tails are made of. They come in multiple colors and sizes. I find the size 2 to be the best all-around size for this one. Because this fly spends most of its time bouncing off rocks on the bottom, I like to make it as durable as possible, so instead of an underbody of dubbing, I use EP Wooly Critter Brushes. They have a wire core, so they're extremely durable. I like the stiffness of the round rubber legs for this fly—maybe it's my OCD, or maybe I just like straight lines, but the round rubber stays straighter while still moving a lot in the water.

In the past, I've tied these only with medium lead eyes, but in recent years, as my subsurface game has evolved toward lighter flies, I started tying them with small or extra-small lead eyes. Typically, on any given day, I'll have these tied with three different-size lead eyes. If I need to fish them in slower-moving shallow water, I'll use the smaller eyes, but if I'm fishing in faster-moving water with some depth, I'll stick with the medium eyes. There's a fine line

The dobsonfly, the adult version of a hellgrammite, is just as terrifying.

between donating these flies to the river and getting them down to the right depth. Heavy doesn't always work, so it's best to have them in a few different sizes.

The hellgrammite fly is a must-have in every smallmouth angler's box. It doesn't have to be this one, but I promise you, if you have them, they work!

FISHING TECHNIQUES

Most of the time, I fish Crittermites in fast water, either swinging them or fishing them under an indicator. Fast water doesn't always mean riffly water either. If the water shallows up and there are a lot of rocks, but the water is still moving quickly, toss a hellgrammite in and swing it. If you find deeper holes, cast it up toward the top and let it fall into the hole. Don't strip it, just pick up the slack as it gets closer to you. Tumbling and rolling around is very natural for these bugs, so imitate that with your presentation.

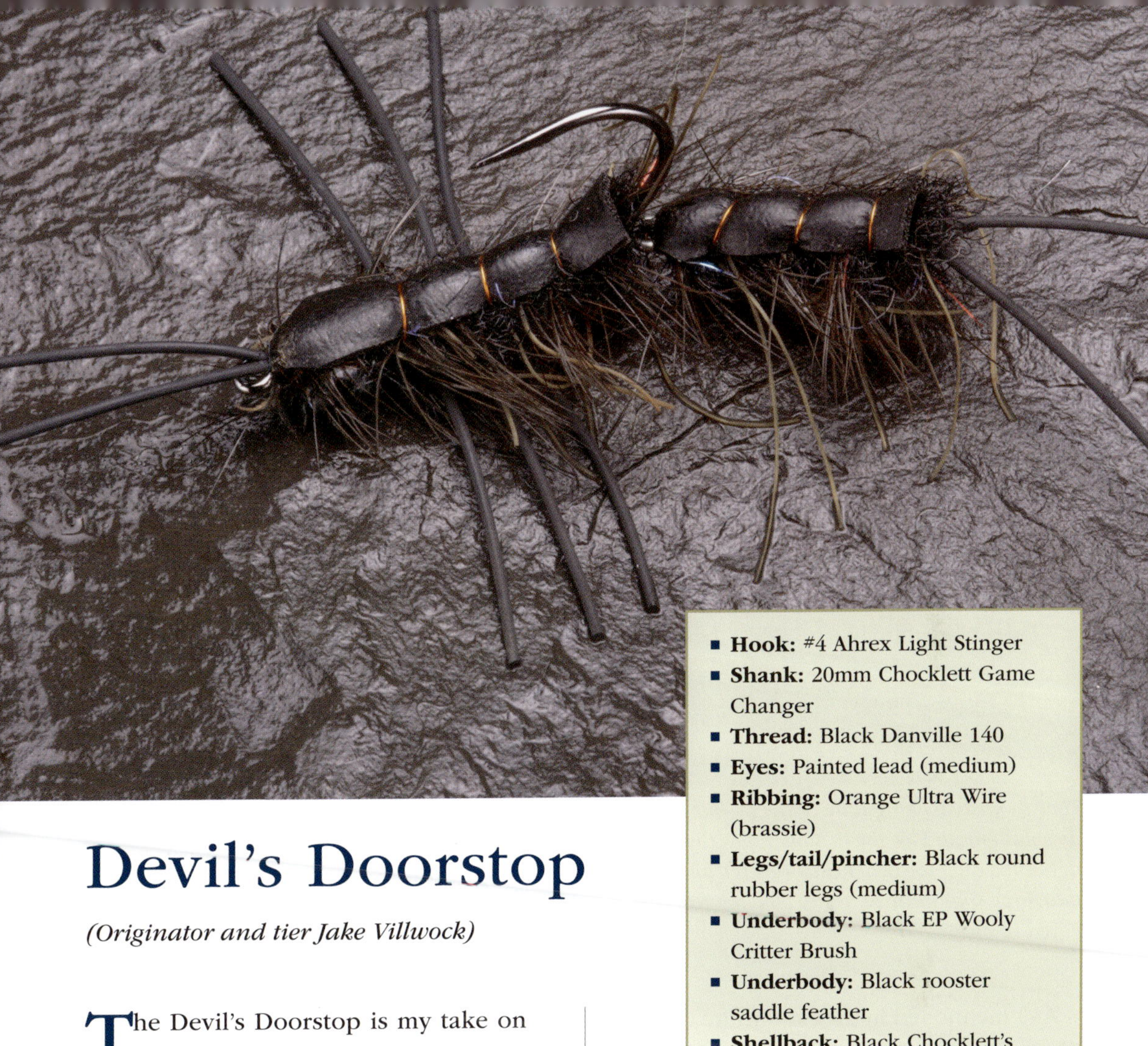

Devil's Doorstop

(Originator and tier Jake Villwock)

- **Hook:** #4 Ahrex Light Stinger
- **Shank:** 20mm Chocklett Game Changer
- **Thread:** Black Danville 140
- **Eyes:** Painted lead (medium)
- **Ribbing:** Orange Ultra Wire (brassie)
- **Legs/tail/pincher:** Black round rubber legs (medium)
- **Underbody:** Black EP Wooly Critter Brush
- **Underbody:** Black rooster saddle feather
- **Shellback:** Black Chocklett's Foam Skin

The Devil's Doorstop is my take on a hellgrammite nymph. It got its name because I think these things are nasty, gross, and just mean. But hey, smallmouth love them, so I can't hate them too much!

With the advancements in tying materials like Blane Chocklett's shanks and gummy foam, we no longer have to rely on rabbit Zonkers or ostrich herl to achieve movement and length for larger nymphs, as was common in many of the original patterns by guides and tiers like Harry Murray and Michael Verduin. We can now articulate these flies, which not only adds movement but also allows us to achieve the desired size.

The Devil's Doorstop is an articulated hellgrammite fly that shines in the summer months. The articulation adds just the right amount of movement, making it perfect for slow retrieves, enticing smallmouth with its lifelike action.

They're nasty-looking little critters—but man, do smallmouth love them. Sometimes the uglier the bug, the better it works. It's all about matching that natural, gritty vibe the fish are keyed in on.

As I mentioned in the Crittermite chapter, I love how that fly fishes, but I couldn't find a good way to articulate it without creating a larger gap or filling that gap with unnecessary materials. So, I started looking into other options. I tried tying it with regular thin fly foam, but it got chewed up too quickly and started to tear off. Then I remembered Blane had a stretchy foam material, so I tried that out. Problem solved—it was durable and gave me the shellback consistency I was looking for, and it was much denser than regular foam, so it withstood the abuse from smallmouth.

I wanted the fly to look buggy, so instead of just using Wooly Critter Brush with the micro legs, I palmered rooster saddle over it like a Woolly Bugger, securing it with Ultra Wire that also doubled as ribbing for the foam back. Round rubber legs were a must, so I took the same configuration from the Crittermite and added it to this one.

Much like Blane's Hellgrammite Changer, you can make this fly as big as you want. Sometimes, I'll keep the hook and shank the same and just add one more shank off the back, so it's not a Changer, but it's articulated twice. It's a bit of a pain to tie with multiple articulations, but the added movement is worth it. However, the combination of rooster saddle, Wooly Critter Brush, and rubber legs gives it plenty of movement on its own, so there's no need to add more if you don't want to.

Hellgrammites are an important part of the smallmouth's diet, and I would say they are genetically wired to look for them. When I first started guiding, I couldn't find a hellgrammite nymph and I never saw a dobsonfly in the air, but smallmouth didn't seem to care. It was a food source they were familiar with, and they ate it.

FISHING TECHNIQUES

There are a few different ways you can fish the Devil's Doorstop. One way is just like fishing a crayfish: casting it up and mending while picking up the slack. Another way is fishing it under an indicator in faster water. Although, as many times as I've tried it, I can't say it works any better than just fishing it and watching the end of your line.

The third way I fish it is as part of a double streamer rig. I'll fish this trailing behind a crayfish or sculpin pattern or run it on top with a smaller nymph like a stonefly or Hex nymph trailing behind it. The double streamer technique is great when you need to get down deeper but don't have many different weight options in your flies.

Red Eye Leech

(Originator and tier Mike Schultz)

The Red Eye Leech is a simple yet effective fly pattern, particularly for smallmouth bass. It's also one of the first commercially available flies from Mike Schultz—and for good reason. Leeches aren't often discussed when it comes to smallmouth forage. You hear about them for trout, especially in lakes, but many rivers where smallmouth reside are home to leeches too. Since smallmouth are known to consume nearly anything, leeches are definitely on the menu.

In many freshwater systems, leeches thrive in the shallow, warmer waters with little current. Two common types found across the eastern and middle United States are the turtle leech and the North American medical leech. Many

Leeches often fly under the radar in fishing conversations, but they're a common presence in nearly all warmwater fisheries. What makes leech flies especially effective is their versatility—not only do they resemble leeches in their natural form, but they're also easily mistaken for worms, making them an excellent all-around pattern for smallmouth bass. The Red Eye Leech is a prime example, perfectly mimicking the look and movement of these overlooked but highly productive critters.

anglers have likely seen a flat, slimy critter while flipping over rocks, perhaps not realizing it's a leech—this is the turtle leech. Its round, flat body is distinct. The other common leech, the traditional long, slender type, is the North American medical leech. These critters often reside in the same areas smallmouth hunt, especially in the summer, making leeches a prime food source.

In Pennsylvania rivers, turtle leeches can often be found near the banks, where dead wood and sand create the perfect habitat. These areas are also great for crayfish and stonecats, so smallmouth are always in the vicinity, ready to feast on whatever they can find—including leeches.

The Red Eye Leech comes in various sizes, with the larger variant displayed here. Mike ties this larger version for winter fishing when he needs to get the fly down quickly and keep it there. This pattern features large lead eyes, a tungsten cone, a rabbit tail, and a palmered rabbit body. A bit of red and gold flash accents the fly, and a mallard flank collar adds contrast, while the head is made of rabbit-spun dubbing. It's a simple fly, but it works.

Commercially tied versions tend to be smaller, better suited for summer fishing. When I tie them, I use small or extra-small lead eyes and size 4 hooks. These lighter versions help me fish in shallow, skinny water, where smaller rocks and less current prevail. A lighter fly allows me to navigate over rocks and around deadfall near the banks more effectively.

While black is a reliable color, especially for larger leeches fished in high, off-color water, I prefer olive, brown, or tan for summer fishing. These colors mimic the leeches I encounter in warmer months.

FISHING TECHNIQUES

In winter, when the water is higher, I typically fish the larger Red Eye Leech with floating lines. Longer leaders help get the fly down but keep the line above the water, allowing me to mend and slow the drift. The tip of the fly line also acts as an indicator.

In summer, I use the same approach, even in shallow water. Floating lines let me slow down the presentation, allowing the fly to sink at the fish's pace or in response to the water's flow. Whether in high or low water, this technique provides an effective and consistent presentation.

River Crawler

(Originator and tier Jake Villwock)

- **Hook:** #4 Ahrex Light Stinger
- **Thread:** Fluorescent chartreuse Danville 140
- **Eyes:** Chartreuse/white/black Hareline Double Pupil Lead Eyes
- **Underbody:** Sculpin EP Wooly Critter Brush
- **Tail/body/head:** Olive barred rabbit Zonker
- **Collar:** Pepperoni Senyo's Aqua Veil
- **Collar:** Olive barred schlappen feather
- **Legs:** Avocado/orange Wapsi Barred Fire Tip Sili Legs

Originally named the Orange Belly River Crawler, this fly began as a way to incorporate an orange accent into all of my subsurface patterns, inspired by the orange accents found on every crayfish. I first tied it with fluorescent orange EP Wooly Critter Brush for the underbody, and it worked great in faster or murkier water. However, I noticed that when the water was at its typical summer flows, I saw more bass swimming away from it than swimming toward it. That's when I decided it was time to tone it down, making it a subtler fly more suited to summer fishing conditions.

To achieve a less intrusive look, I removed the orange and replaced it with a color closer to the rabbit Zonker wing.

The River Crawler isn't just a leech—it can imitate a variety of forage species for smallmouth. The rubber legs not only enhance the movement but also add to the profile, making it resemble not just a leech but also a smaller baitfish.

However, I still wanted the fly to have a little pop. So, instead of the solid orange underbody, I opted to use Barred Fire Tip Sili Legs. This gives the fly movement when stationary and a subtle hint of orange—enough to catch attention without overpowering the presentation.

I tie these on a size 4 Ahrex light stinger hook with small lead eyes. As mentioned earlier, leeches typically inhabit shallow, warm water with little to no current, so a heavy fly isn't necessary. I also add two wraps of Senyo's Aqua Veil in "pepperoni," a red and green blend, for a touch of color and contrast. A barred schlappen feather adds structure and enhances the fly's movement, completing the look.

This fly has been a day-saver for me during the summer months, especially when the crayfish bite is slow. Even when crayfish aren't the primary food source, I can always pick up fish with this leech pattern by fishing it slowly along the edges. I typically tie it in olive or tan, but brown is also effective, depending on the bottom color. Olive works

A baby hog sucker

best in rocky areas, while tan is ideal for sandy or woody bottom habitats.

What makes this fly so versatile is that it can imitate not only leeches but also smaller sculpins, darters, and baby hog suckers. The slender profile, the eyes, and the barred rabbit Zonker (when wet) all resemble these other forage species that smallmouth love. The rubber legs act as pectoral fins, adding realism to the presentation.

This is why I don't simply call it a "leech" pattern. Though it's certainly effective as a leech imitation, it's really more of a "River Crawler" because it's a jack-of-all-trades. It imitates multiple prey species, making it a must-have fly for any smallmouth angler.

FISHING TECHNIQUES

For almost all of my presentations, I prefer fishing this fly with a floating line. If you use a sinking line of any rate, it becomes much harder to mend the line and slow the presentation effectively. Additionally, detecting a strike is more difficult when the line is subsurface. A sinking line creates a large surface area that the water can pull downstream faster than desired, causing the fly to move too quickly or erratically.

The front/top view of this fly showcases its natural taper, resembling either a leech or a baitfish.

By using a floating line, you can cast toward structure in slower water and crawl the fly back at a controlled pace. If you're wade fishing, swinging the fly downstream is also a good technique. However, be sure to throw in a few mends to slow the drift down, keeping the fly in the strike zone for longer.

Always keep an eye on the tip of your fly line for any sudden stops or pauses. These subtle signals often indicate a strike, and being attentive will help you detect them more easily.

INDEX